Unlocking the Kingdom

Key Principles to Release God's Kingdom Power

By

Mark Hoffman

ISBN#: 978-159352-432-6

Printed by
Christian Services Network
1975 Janich Ranch Ct.
El Cajon, CA 92019
Toll Free: 1-866-484-6184
www.csnbooks.com

Printed in the United States of America

Breakthrough Kingdom Living was first published in October, 1994; Revised, Second Printing: November, 1999 Third Printing: March, 2005

Fourth Printing, 2008, under new title, **Unlocking the Kingdom**, and includes revised and expanded Discussion Questions.

Dedication

This book is dedicated to all the followers of Jesus Christ who *"seek first His kingdom and His righteousness"* (Matthew 6:33). A broken, weary and increasingly hopeless world waits upon our maturing and promotion.

> *As for the saints who are in the earth, They are the majestic ones in whom is all my delight.*
>
> (Psalm 16:3)

Table of Contents

Introduction

It is a privilege to share the principles of this book with you, the reader. Although for some they may appear elementary, there are many others who are like I was some years ago. I had only a vague understanding of exactly what the Kingdom of God was, or how it operated. Further, there was no one who took me aside and taught me the basic principles of God's Kingdom in a systematic way. I made many mistakes early in my Christian life simply out of ignorance.

I am indebted to Pat Robertson for writing his book, *The Secret Kingdom* (which I highly recommend). It introduced me to the concept that there were principles by which God's Kingdom operated. Since reading that book some twenty-five years ago, I have endeavored to explore this concept by biblical study and by putting the principles into action in the laboratory of life. By the grace of God I have tried to live as faithfully as possible to these principles over the past twenty-five years, neither turning from them to the left or to the right (Joshua 1:7). I began my study and apprenticeship to these Kingdom principles when I literally had nothing; I was totally stripped and felt absolutely defeated.

This book is not a theoretical or intellectual exercise, but a testimony to the truth of these principles as I have discovered them. I therefore make no apologies for the many personal references throughout the book. It is to the application of these principles alone, and not any native talent, natural advantage, or fortunate circumstance that I point for any measure of success I might enjoy today. These experiences prove that by following God's directions, even a dark horse can know victory! It is my firm conviction that these principles will equally prove themselves in the life of anyone who simply will take God at His word and employ them.

Certainly this book does not pretend to be an exhaustive list of all of the principles or keys to the Kingdom, nor do I even claim that these are the most important. It does, however, give a starting point to living a true Kingdom lifestyle which will bear great fruit in the lives of those who employ it.

This book is meant to be used as a handbook, a reference to be reviewed again and again over the years until the principles contained within it become part of your habit. It is written out of the conviction that Jesus Christ is currently reigning over all the affairs of mankind, and wants to reign through those who have taken His yoke upon themselves and learned from Him. This book serves as a companion to another of my books, *On Earth as It Is in Heaven* (information on ordering is available at the end of this book). Together these two books will give you an overview of God's Kingdom and how to enter it and enjoy its riches and power.

These chapters were originally written for use in our church's home study groups. I've included the discussion questions used in those small groups. Perhaps this book is best suited to small group use where the participants can discuss the principles fully and encourage each other week by week to put them into practice. The chapters can be read at home prior to the meeting, or read together as a group. Many of the groups read only half a chapter each week.

It is imperative for the Church to understand the principles of God's Kingdom so we might bring reformation to our culture and our country. It is out of this conviction that I offer to the Church this feeble attempt to stimulate it toward its own greatness.

1

Inheriting the Kingdom

From atop a high hill, Joshua shielded his eyes from the early morning sun. Stretching before him, just across the Jordan River, was the Promised Land. Straining his eyes to see as far as possible, he surveyed the lush richness of the Jordan River Valley stretching out before him.

It was just as he remembered it.

A rich land, a land flowing with milk and honey.

It had all seemed so simple on that day forty years ago when he returned with the twelve other spies to report to Moses of their reconnaissance of the land. If God had promised them the land, then He would certainly give it to them. That is what he believed and that is the report he stuck with, despite the arguments of ten of the other spies and the fear of the people.

Of course, Moses was his leader then. It was easy to be brave and full of faith around Moses. Moses had been their rock. Had any person ever known God as he had? He was always so strong and certain. Raised in the very palace of Pharaoh, educated in all the knowledge of the world, and called by the very Presence of God in a burning bush, he had spoken to God face to face and received the tablets of the Law, written by the very finger of God. Moses had called the ten plagues down upon the Egyptians, parted the Red Sea, and caused water to flow from a rock.

It was easy to believe anything when you were around Moses.

But Moses was dead.

After forty years, he would no longer be the voice to lead the people.

Now it would be Joshua's voice.

Joshua already knew his first assignment. Moses himself had said in the hearing of all the people:

Go now and take the promised land for the Lord your God will dispossess these nations before you, and will certainly give it to you, and Joshua is the one who will cross the Jordan ahead of you.

(Deuteronomy 31:3)

But which way should they go?

How should they wage war?

The Canaanites, who lived in the land, were among the most skilled and fearsome of all peoples in warfare.

Joshua looked across the Jordan River Valley; less than ten miles away was the great walled city of Jericho rising up out of the valley like an insurmountable obstacle. Its massive double walls were said to be unconquerable.

Even if you could scale or breach the outer wall, you would be trapped between it and the second wall. For centuries it had been a locked door to anyone wanting to invade Canaan from the east.

But it was not the war and battles that most worried Joshua...a greater concern occupied his mind.

He was no longer the young man, merely forty days out of slavery to Egypt, who had gone in to scout the land nearly forty years earlier. Then it had seemed so easy to go in and be in a new nation in a new land.

He had been so naive.

His life as a slave had not prepared him for the difficulties and pitfalls of the birth of a society. He had been blinded to it all by his enthusiasm and zeal. However, forty years of assisting Moses in leading this people in their desert wanderings had given him a taste of the impossible task that awaited him.

How could a nation of ex-slaves who had no experience in building a society, establishing an economy, a banking system or a system of national security, or of even running a city, ever hope to accomplish it all...and prosper?

How did 400 years of making bricks as slave laborers, and then forty years of nomadic wandering in the desert, prepare them to establish a nation among all the other hostile nations of the earth?

How could they, thoroughly unprepared as they were, ever hope to achieve lasting success even if they did defeat and destroy the Canaanites?

Joshua was shaken out of his thoughts by a voice. Or was it a voice? Did he actually hear it? There it was again. Joshua sat in sheer terror as he heard the very voice of God.

Moses my servant is dead; now therefore arise, cross this Jordan, you and all this people, to the land which I am giving to them, to the sons of Israel. Every place on which the sole of your foot treads, I have given it to you, just as I spoke to Moses...No man will be able to stand before you all the days of your life. Just as I have been with Moses, I will be with you; I will not fail you or forsake you. Be strong and courageous, for you shall give this people possession of the land which I swore to their fathers to give them

(Joshua 1:2-3, 5-6)

And then came the words that would answer all of Joshua's doubts and questions, the words that would give him the wisdom and strategy for the impossible task.

Only be strong and very courageous; be careful to do according to all the law which Moses My servant commanded you; do not turn from it to the right or to the left, so that you may have success wherever you go. This book of the law shall not depart from your mouth, but you shall meditate on it day and night, so that you may be careful to do according to all that is written in it; for then you will make your way prosperous, and then you will have success.

(Joshua 1:7-8)

Of course, Joshua suddenly realized, God has already given them the key to success! It was contained in the laws God had given Moses. The very principles and wisdom that had guided them in the wilderness would establish their kingdom and society!

Moses had written down all these laws and precepts in a book (Deuteronomy 31:24). That book contained the secret keys by which all of life operated. If they would be careful to learn and put into practice the laws and principles contained in that book, then they would always know God's Presence and they would succeed and prosper no matter what the circumstances or obstacles. It was as if God had given them the secret blueprint for how the world operates, and how to succeed in it.

History records that Joshua and the next generation were careful to follow the directions and laws contained in the Law that God had given to Moses. As a result, a kingdom was established that lasted for over 800 years and became, under David and Solomon, the greatest kingdom in all the Mideast. It was only after the Law of God was abandoned, and idolatry was embraced, that the kingdom was lost centuries later.

Like Joshua, we too face the prospect of conquering a hostile land inhabited by giants. Violence, prejudice, lust, deception, unbelief, rebellion, rage, addiction, perversion and apathy rule our land, sometimes even invading our homes.

These are formidable enemies.

But we must do more than simply war against such forces...we must construct lives, marriages, families, churches and a whole society that is godly, righteous and successful. We must displace failing structures, systems and philosophies with new ones that are godly.

But how can we ever defeat such foes, let alone build something constructive to take their places?

Like Joshua, we have the same answers from the same source - the Bible.

All around us we see major institutions falling, and men's hearts beginning to fail them out of fear. Schools have become dens of violence and immorality, Congress and state legislatures have become corrupted, our streets are unsafe, our families are crumbling, and the glue that holds society together seems to have disappeared. What is worse, those in established places of power seem unable to do anything about any of it!

But it simply will not do for God's people to sit around wringing their hands when He has given us a Kingdom that cannot be shaken. God has us on this earth not to worry but to war, not to be conquered but to conquer, not to be irrelevant but to be the very salt of the earth.

God has enabled us to triumph by giving us His very Presence to be our light and strength, and His Word to be our strategy and guide. By walking with Him and carefully following His Word, neither turning *"from it to the right or to the left"* and by being *"careful to do according to all that is written in it,"* we too can also make our way to prosperity and success.

The Old and New Testaments give us keys to the rule of God among men, which we call the Kingdom of God. In the chapters that follow we will study this eternal, invisible Kingdom and learn the practical principles we can follow to release God's blessing and bounty into our lives, marriages, families, churches, cities and nation. The power and authority to prosper and overcome is still ours today if we will realize the importance of knowing and following God's Word fully. Although many today treat the study of God's Word as optional, knowing His Word is in fact essential to our very life, as Moses told the Israelites in his final address to them.

> *For it is not an idle word for you; indeed it is your life. And by this word you will prolong your days in the land, which you are about to cross the Jordan to possess.*
>
> (Deuteronomy 32:47)

2

The Secret Keys to the Kingdom

Jesus told His followers not to focus on the things that the Gentiles or the unbelievers sought. In Matthew 6:25-32, Jesus spoke of how people worried about such things as:

- having enough to eat and drink

- having clothing to wear

- the length of their lives and their health

- worries about the future.

It would seem that things have not changed much since then. Certainly it seems normal to worry about these things. After all, who hasn't spent a sleepless night worrying about how to make a mortgage payment, find employment before the savings run out, or find enough extra money to fix the car? Who hasn't tossed and turned the night before taking a physical or getting a lab report back?

Although these seem like very normal concerns, Jesus forbids His followers from being focused on such things. He said *"do not be worried about your life"* (Matthew 6:25). Jesus taught them principles that would ensure abundance in all these areas through bringing them into God's superabundance. Jesus said,

> *Do not worry, then…But seek first His kingdom and His righteousness, and all these things* (the material concerns) *will be added to you.*
> (Matthew 6:31, 33)

Jesus said there is an invisible realm, an unseen Kingdom, a spiritual reality greater than the physical realm you know. When you enter into this Kingdom and begin to understand how it functions, it will bring with it all earthly blessings.

The invisible undergirds and governs the visible.

Jesus spent the three years of His earthly ministry living by these Kingdom principles. He was never limited by the physical, but understood how to release God's blessing and bounty into human need. He not only demonstrated these principles or keys to the Kingdom, He also taught His followers how to live by them.

Jesus taught more on the Kingdom of God than any other subject.

When Jesus said to the apostle Peter, *"I will give you the keys of the kingdom of heaven"* (Matthew 16:19), He was giving Peter more than just apostolic authority. He was also promising to give him teaching and insight into how this invisible, secret Kingdom operated.

Today individuals, families and whole societies are being defeated by seemingly insurmountable problems. Marriages and families drift apart and self-destruct, men and women fall again and again in defeat to addictions and compulsions, debts rise higher, young people grow aimless, crime and misery mount, and individuals and even whole governments seem unable to fix the situation.

Increasingly, people are desperate!

The answer to overcoming these problems is to learn how to reach into the superabundance and possibilities of God by using the keys to the Kingdom that Jesus gave us. God is eager to bring His infinite potential and possibilities into the realm of our human limitation and weakness through our obedient and faithful application of these Kingdom principles. These principles or laws are absolutely essential to our happiness and success. Those who fail to learn and follow these Kingdom directives, even Christians, will fail to experience the deliverance and help that is available to them.

UNDERSTANDING SPIRITUAL LAW

Why are these laws so important? Remember that the universe or cosmos was created by an orderly and law-creating God. All around us we see, amidst the tremendous complexity, a perfect order. This great order is because everything in the universe is governed by great laws which we call laws of nature.

These great laws cannot be ignored.

Learning them has been the key to man's progress.

But Creation, or "the created order," is made up of more than that which is visible. There is more to it than that which we can see or feel or smell or hear. God's created order includes both things in the physical and spiritual realm, things both visible and invisible:

For by Him all things were created, both in the heavens and on earth, visible and invisible…

(Colossians 1:16)

The invisible spiritual world includes such things as angels, demons, ruling spiritual powers, faith, love, hope, the Holy Spirit, visions, fear, joy, guilt, forgiveness, spiritual power, blessing, cursing, witchcraft, influence, inspiration, peace, self-concept, unity, plus much more! The same God who created the physical world and governs it by laws also created the invisible and spiritual world and likewise governs it by laws that we call spiritual law.

God's Creation, whether visible or invisible, is consistent. Both are governed by law because God is an orderly and law-creating God. These two realms, the physical and the spiritual, correspond to each other and are interconnected. In fact, the Bible tells us the physical world, which came later, was created out of the spiritual world.

By faith we understand that the worlds were prepared by the word of God, so that what is seen was not made out of things which are visible.

(Hebrews 11:3)

By faith - by believing God - we know that the world and the stars - in fact, all things - were made at God's command; and that they were all made from things that can't be seen.

(Hebrews 11:3, The Living Bible)

There is an old saying that a river can never flow higher than its source. An orderly, law-abiding physical world could only have come out of an orderly, law-abiding spiritual world. It is a temporary embodiment or expression of the spiritual world.

For the things which are seen are temporary, but the things which are not seen are eternal.

(2 Corinthians 4:18, NKJ)

Most Christians recognize that physical or natural laws are always in operation and are sure and certain. Yet many of those same Christians apparently do not believe that the same is true of moral or spiritual laws. The Bible, however, makes no such distinction.

Can a man take fire in his bosom And his clothes not be burned? Or can a man walk on hot coals And his feet not be scorched? So is the one who goes in to his neighbor's wife; Whoever touches her will not go unpunished.

(Proverbs 6:27-29)

The first two questions above are questions of simple physics. The third reflects spiritual physics. God takes pains here to assure us that each result is equally certain. Spiritual law is no less certain than natural law.

Furthermore, because the physical world came out of the spiritual, there is a close correspondence between the operations of the physical world and those of the spiritual world. This explains why Jesus' favorite way to teach about the principles in the spiritual world was to correlate them to laws and principles we observe operating in nature and the normal affairs of people. These comparisons we call *parables.* The New Testament records thirty parables of Jesus.

For instance, the way a tiny mustard seed grows into a huge bush illustrates the potential of even a tiny amount of faith to grow and accomplish great things.

The way yeast operates in bread corresponds to the way sin operates in an individual life or fellowship.

The laws and operations of the physical world mirror the laws and operations of the spiritual world.

This means that the abundance and possibilities of God's Kingdom are available to those who follow God's spiritual laws in the same way that the natural world has yielded its richness to scientific, modern man who has learned and harnessed the great laws of nature.

Think about it.

Try to imagine what life was like on planet earth before man began to scientifically study and apply the laws of the physical world to bring about technology and progress. Although mankind was surrounded by the tremendous potential and riches of our world, they were untapped, and people lived in great want. There was no electric power because man did not understand the potential power flowing in water or wind. The use of airplanes, vaccines and telephones had to wait until man understood the natural laws that would make them possible, and then harnessed them to work for him.

Norway has more flowing water than any place in the world. Electricity is so plentiful and inexpensive due to the copious amounts of hydroelectric power generated by their many rivers that they never bother to turn off their lights. Yet, in ancient Norway, the Vikings lived by candlelight and relied on cooking fires because they were ignorant to the potential around them. They did not understand the principle of electricity.

The same is true in the spiritual world.

People are suffering today because they do not understand God's great laws, and they are ignorant of the tremendous potential and power available. Today, most suffering is caused, not by ignorance of the natural world, but because of ignorance or disobedience to the spiritual laws of the invisible world. Even Christians can be ignorant of God's Kingdom principles and suffer great want.

Many Christians assume that if they are well-intentioned, God will spare them from the consequences of ignorance. Many do not consider it important to really know and master God's Word and its principles. Every day they act and make decisions from a worldly mindset, not understanding the spiritual principles and laws involved.

But, if God will not spare well-intentioned Christians who violate natural laws like gravity or combustion, what makes us think He will suspend the cause and effect of law in the spiritual and moral realms because we have been too lazy to study? In fact, the Bible tells us just the opposite:

My people are destroyed for lack of knowledge.

(Hosea 4:6)

MAKE LIFE WORK FOR YOU INSTEAD OF AGAINST YOU

A Christian living in ignorance or disobedience of spiritual law will suffer just as much as a Christian living in ignorance or disobedience to natural laws like that of gravity or hygiene. Christians harm their walk with God, themselves, their marriages and children by violating spiritual principles, sometimes unknowingly.

Ignorance is no excuse!

Nor can they say "Well, God knows my heart. He knows I was doing my best." (Of course they weren't doing their best, since they weren't pursuing instruction and knowledge.) Being naive or being too busy to know God's Word comes at a heavy price.

And you neglected all my counsel And did not want my reproof...Because they hated knowledge And did not choose the fear of the Lord So they shall eat of the fruit of their own way And be satiated with their own devices. For the waywardness of the naive will kill them.

(Proverbs 1:25, 29, 31-32)

God has revealed spiritual laws to us through His Word, the Bible. These principles, when humbly and faithfully applied in dependence upon God, can deliver us from afflictions and bring us into God's richness.

He sent His Word and healed them, And delivered them from all their destructions.

(Psalm 107:20)

This book of the law shall not depart from your mouth, but you shall meditate on it day and night, so that you may be careful to do according to all that is written in it; for then you will make your way prosperous, and then you will have success.

(Joshua 1:8)

Natural law has a direct effect upon the physical world.

Spiritual law has a direct effect upon your spiritual, moral and emotional state and indirectly (but no less powerfully) upon the natural world.

For instance, a person's understanding of the law of stewardship will directly affect his spiritual experience of God, but will also affect his financial situation, since the dynamic of God's blessing and provision is affected. Following these principles will have a greater effect upon our life than all the events and circumstances that life can throw at us. Jesus promised His followers that by hearing and following His teachings, they could build their houses (i.e., lives) on a solid rock that would endure and prosper even during the worst storm (Matthew 7:24-27).

Most Christians love Jesus, but know almost nothing about the Kingdom Jesus talked so much about, and even less about the principles and laws that open it up to people. As you diligently study and apply these Kingdom principles, or keys, you will just as certainly see benefits and results as those who apply the natural laws in the physical world.

My son, give attention to my words; Incline your ear to my sayings. Do not let them depart from your sight; Keep them in the midst of your heart. For they are life to those who find them And health to all their whole body.

(Proverbs 4:20-22)

3

The Kingdom Key of Thanksgiving and Praise

Shout joyfully to the LORD, all the earth. Enter His gates with thanksgiving And His courts with praise…

(Psalm 100:1, 4)

This psalm gives us a glimpse of the profound truth about God, and a powerful key to His Kingdom. God is pictured here as a king ruling over His Kingdom from His walled city or temple. Before one can come into God's presence, one must gain access to the walled area.

But how? The walls are much too high to scale, and much too thick to dig through. No human can storm God's dwelling place and demand an audience. People can shout to the heavens and even shake fists, but all that comes back is silence.

This verse shows us the pass that gets us through the gates. It is an attitude of thankfulness that brings us into an experience of the Kingdom, and a heart full of praise that brings us into the very court of the King!

The Kingdom Key of Thanksgiving and Praise may be stated in this way: *as we move toward God with an attitude of thanksgiving and praise, He moves toward us with His glorious presence and help.*

Psalm 22:3 in the King James Version tells us God inhabits the praises of His people. God seeks a people who have learned the Kingdom Key of Thanksgiving. He dwells among them.

People who live in a state of thankfulness are people who are always prepared for God's blessing. They are living out God's will and purpose for them.

> *Rejoice always; in everything give thanks; for this is God's will for you in Christ Jesus.*
>
> (1 Thessalonians 5:16, 18)

A POWERFUL PRINCIPLE

Very few Kingdom principles have as immediate and dynamic an effect as learning to live and walk in thanksgiving and praise. The person who walks in thanksgiving will always experience the presence and grace of God. They will experience the Lord's strength and joy even amidst the most trying circumstances. Those who have developed a lifestyle of being thankful to God have made a wonderful discovery: the instant we begin to thank the Lord, we rise out of our weakness into His strength and comfort.

Although we live in the most blessed country in history, recent studies show that eighty-seven percent of Americans dwell on negative thoughts. At no time, in no other place, have people enjoyed the blessings we take for granted. However, as a people our lives are often marked by complaining, anxiousness and bitterness. How few are the people who count their blessings, and how many are angry or bitter over some real or imagined hurt or deprivation!

People are defeated or succeed not so much because of what happens to them but because of the perspective they adopt in evaluating those events. Our perspective largely determines our perceptions and expectations. These, in turn, have a far greater impact on our future happiness and success than any event that has happened in the past.

Our attitude is always the single most important element in any situation. The good news is that while our perspective has a profound effect upon our life, it is something that we are free to choose.

Benjamin Franklin maintained that this one sentence above all others impacted his life: "Some people grumble because God placed thorns among the roses; why not thank God because He placed roses among thorns?" That sentence reflects a change in perspective; a small change that will revolutionize any life: while a person's life may have had great hardships, there were also great blessings from God.

Many people's lives are dominated by anger at a parent, ex-spouse or some other individual believed to have in some way caused them to miss out on something or to be deprived. However, when we allow ourselves to feel this way, we fall into a terrible trap. We ensure our future unhappiness and defeat. We are defeated by what we have *chosen* to make the focal point of our life. Why not focus on things to thank God for? There are blessings and evidences of God's kindness in every life.

When we focus on problems instead of blessings, we feel helpless and overwhelmed, and see ourselves as victims.

Victim-type personalities have it backwards. They take responsibility for what others have done to them in the past but absolve themselves of responsibility for what they are doing or feeling in the present. Many carry guilt because someone else abused them, or carry shame because someone else abandoned them. In so doing, they take responsibility for the sin of someone else. They say "I can't help it. I'm the way I am because of what so-and-so did to me in the past." In this way they claim to be helpless or not responsible for the sinful way they are acting or feeling today.

But the truth is that our future will be determined by the attitudes and perspectives we *choose* to adopt and the decisions and actions we make today. Why not be encouraged by the positive people God brought into our lives along the way? Why not be encouraged by God's faithfulness to us throughout it all?

We seem to spend ninety percent of our time worrying about the ten percent we don't have and ten percent of our time being grateful for the ninety percent we do have. When we do this, we violate the spiritual principle of thanksgiving and give ninety percent of our mind over to destructive and negative thoughts. But when we choose to focus on our blessings and adopt an attitude of thankfulness, God draws close and our thinking becomes productive.

It would seem that thankfulness and gratitude is something that just doesn't come naturally to us. In Luke 17 Jesus healed ten lepers and only one returned to give thanks. The others were so caught up in their blessing that they forgot to give thanks. I guess people don't change much. Even today people probably are still nine times more likely to be ungrateful and take blessings for granted than to be thankful.

Thankfulness just doesn't come naturally to us. We must work at it. We must work at helping our children to be grateful. After all, no one has to teach their kids to say "mine" or "I want" but you do have to patiently teach them to say "Thank you." If you love your kids you will take pains to teach them to be grateful; it is so important to their future well being.

Gratitude and thanksgiving bring life and a blessing; grumbling and complaining bring a curse of deprivation and death. This is the flip side of the principle of thanksgiving.

This is illustrated in God's response to the grumbling and complaining of the Israelites after He led them out of Egypt.

> *How long shall I bear with this evil congregation who are grumbling against me? I have heard the complaints of the sons of Israel, which they are making against Me. Say to them, "As I live," says the Lord, "just as you have spoken in My hearing, so I will surely do to you."*
> (Numbers 14:27-28)

Here we see that although the Israelites would probably later blame God for the bad things that would soon happen, it was really a result of their own attitude. To an extent, they were writing their own prescription. They had said over and over again that the Lord could not deliver them, that they would be defeated, and that their wives and children would be carried off as slaves…despite God's assurances of help and protection! Finally, God said, "Fine, have it your way. You will get what you believe and what you are expecting."

How to Become Fertile Ground

The giving of thanks and a grateful spirit are fertile ground for faith to grow; whereas, doubt and unbelief naturally result from ingratitude and complaining. Remember, faith is always rewarded; whereas, unbelief blocks us from gaining the blessing.

A thankful attitude is important in maintaining right-thinking and a right mental state. A powerful deception enters the mind once we begin blaming others, or complaining and grumbling about our circumstances. It opens our mind to darkness and futility rather than God's truth and light. The book of Romans documents this.

> *For even though they knew God, they did not honor Him as God or give thanks, but they became futile in their speculations, and their foolish heart was darkened.*
>
> (Romans 1:21)

The simple truth is that most depression, anxiety and mental problems stem from an ungrateful heart and a failure to actively thank and praise God. I have learned from personal experience that it is heartfelt praise and thanksgiving alone that can overcome depression and restore us to a right mental perspective. At one point in my own life, when I was a young Christian and in deep despair and confusion, God taught me this Kingdom principle through an older and more mature Christian. As I sat in her house, she told me to stop worrying and fretting about my problems for a few moments and instead begin to thank God out loud for everything I could think of. Of course it was the last thing that I felt like doing, but out of respect for her I began. It started out rather mechanically but soon the thanks and praise were just jumping out of my mouth. Immediately the depression broke, God's peace and joy filled my heart, and I was delivered from a negative, fruitless thought pattern. It was a lesson I never forgot and one I have put into practice many times since then.

I learned that day I could enjoy the power of this principal no matter how I felt - even when I felt like a failure. Remember, thanksgiving and praise depends upon the worthiness of the One receiving it - not the worthiness of the one offering it. Understanding this can help to change your life.

Thanksgiving and praise is like turning your satellite dish right towards God. It puts us on His wave length. It's like God is on the FM frequency and when we grumble, complain, worry and fret we are switched onto the AM signal. When we become grateful and practice thanksgiving, we switch to God's frequency.

Thanksgiving helps you to lay hold of God's great promises.

The practice and expression of thanksgiving and praise is the key missing ingredient for many in laying hold of God's provision for them.

ADDITIONAL THANKSGIVING BENEFITS

Are you anxious and needing God's peace? Thanksgiving and praise will bring God's peace into your life.

Be anxious for nothing, but in everything by prayer and supplication with thanksgiving let your requests be made known to God. And the peace of God, which surpasses all comprehension, will guard your hearts and your minds in Christ Jesus.

(Philippians 4:6-7)

Note that there is a peace available, which is so perfect and so deep that it can "guard our hearts and minds" and it "surpasses all comprehension," because it is able to keep us in perfect peace...even amidst the worst threats and circumstances.

This peace that overcomes anxiety does not merely come by making your requests or needs known through prayer, but, as these verses tell us, by linking prayer with thanksgiving. Many Christians fail to enter this peace during their prayer because, in effect, their prayer is nothing more than complaining, or an expression of their fear and anxiety. They are praying in ignorance or violation of this key that would open the door to peace.

Before you can truly roll your worries onto the Lord's shoulders and receive His "peace that passes understanding," you must come into His courts with thanksgiving and praise. You must continue to sprinkle your petitions with praise and thanksgiving. This will both honor God and bring you before Him with a right attitude and an ignited faith to receive.

Are you spiritually dull; do you struggle with prayer?

Many people report a general failure or lack of discipline in spiritual practices. Although they desire a vital, personal devotional life with the Lord, they feel dull and dead. The principle of praise and thanksgiving can ensure spiritual alertness and increase spiritual capacity. Colossians 4:2 gives us this important secret: *"Devote yourselves to prayer, keeping alert in it with an attitude of thanksgiving."*

Spiritual alertness and sensitivity is developed through giving thanks. Not only prayer, but all spiritual activity is vitalized by the practice of thanksgiving. Learning to thank and praise God gives us a prophetic ability to begin to see the hand of God all around us because an attitude of thankfulness motivates us to develop the skill of looking for what the Lord is doing in every situation...so we can thank Him! Failure to develop this skill leads to an inability to see God's workings and a dullness to God Himself. As we insert thanksgivings amidst our prayer requests and petitions, we are reminded of the Lord's faithfulness, and our faith is ignited to believe for the things we are now requesting.

Do you struggle with sins of the tongue?

Does your mouth get you into trouble? Many people's tongues seem out of control. They have habits of foul language, gossip or a critical tongue. Perhaps they have struggled to overcome them, but with limited success.

The law or principle of thanksgiving can work for them here.

And there must be no filthiness and silly talk, or coarse jesting, which are not fitting, but rather giving of thanks.

(Ephesians 5:4)

Here is a truth I have come to learn from experience. The mouth cannot be filled with both thanksgiving and worthless talk. The more we dedicate our speech to the expression of thanks and the giving of praise, the more we will displace gossip, slander, cursing and criticism.

Giving thanks is an antidote to verbal bondage.

As you can see, like all the kingdom principles, the principle of praise and thanksgiving is a powerful one that, whether recognized or not, exerts a powerful effect on people's lives. God wants you to become a grateful child of His and let this powerful principle work for you. I know of few practices or disciplines that will yield as immediate an impact on your life.

Remember, we read that we were to *"Rejoice always; in everything give thanks; for this is God's will for you in Christ Jesus"* (1 Thessalonians 5:16, 18). God's will in every circumstance is that we give thanks and so receive His strength and overcome. In every situation we can make the choice to be thankful.

Mom, when you look at the sink which is full of dirty dinner dishes you can complain or you can choose to thank God that you had food to prepare and a family to prepare it for.

If you have a blowout on the freeway you can thank God for keeping you from injury. You can thank him that you even have a car and for the spare tire in your trunk.

If you get called to school because your child is misbehaving you can remember that your child is a gift from God and give Him thanks. Further, you can be grateful that your child is still at an age where you have the opportunity to guide him. Believe me, many parents wish they had the chance to do it over.

In every situation you can give thanks, and if you do you will be blessed and you will be an overcomer. Do it and you will see for yourself.

4

The Kingdom Key of a Hidden Life With God

Beware of practicing your righteousness before men to be noticed by them; otherwise you have no reward with your Father who is in heaven. But when you give to the poor, do not let your left hand know what your right hand is doing, so that your giving will be in secret; and your Father who sees what is done in secret will reward you. But you, when you pray, go into your inner room, close your door and pray to your Father who is in secret, and your Father who sees what is done in secret will reward you .

(Matthew 6:1, 2-4, 6)

These verses contain a truth that is an essential key to the practice of a living and vital Christianity. All of our religious practices must have as their chief end to please God and to grow in the direct knowledge of Him. While this might seem obvious, it's just as true that many people are missing the obvious. For instance, people come to church for many other reasons than to meet God. Some come primarily to find acceptance and make friends with nice people. Others want a positive experience that will give them an emotional lift during the week and make them feel better about themselves. Some hope to get some practical help with their marriage or raising their kids.

One of the tragic ironies of modern church life is that many people do seem to forget about God in their practice of religion. Although they may be quite involved in church activities, they have little direct knowledge of God. Their religious practice is meant to demonstrate to themselves or others that they are good and respectable people.

Religion practiced for the approval of man is devoid of power, but religion practiced to please God alone receives a reward.

True Christianity must be forever focused first on the relationship of the individual to his Creator or heavenly Father. Our Father created us in His own image and likeness so we might relate directly to Him and reflect His glory and excellence.

The purpose of Christ's coming was not primarily to save us from sin or hell or deliver us from sickness or even to get us to heaven. These were merely consequences of His true purpose, which was to restore us to our relationship with our Creator and Father.

For it was the Father's good pleasure for all the fullness to dwell in Him, and through Him to reconcile all things to himself, having made peace through the blood of the cross. He has now reconciled you in His fleshly body through death in order to present you before Him holy and blameless and beyond reproach

(Colossians 1:19-22)

The great goal and point of religion is that you grow in knowledge, intimacy and experience of God through Jesus Christ; that you find in God the source of your every need so He becomes your source of security, identity and happiness. As you do this, God's great power and love will become yours. You will find the joy and transforming power that is in true religion.

However, amidst the demands and busyness of everyday life and with an abundance of churches and programs to sample, it's easy to stay busy and not notice that we aren't growing spiritually. It's easy to settle for being outwardly religious instead of becoming truly spiritual.

True Christianity has a secret, hidden side, the soul's growth in direct knowledge, dependence and trust in God. Too many people nullify the power of religion by following the mistake of the Pharisees and practicing their religion toward men rather than toward God.

> *When you pray, you are not to be like the hypocrites; for they love to stand and pray in the synagogues and on the street corners so that they may be seen by men. Truly I say to you, they have their reward in full.*
> (Matthew 6:5)

Prayer practiced toward God gains a reward.

Prayer (or church attendance) practiced to impress others has no divine response or reward. The only reward is the one that was sought - to impress people. The hypocrites Jesus was speaking of had nullified the true power of religion by violating this key principle: **Only a hidden life with God unlocks the true power of religion.**

A truly spiritual Christian who walks in the peace, joy and power of God is like an iceberg. While he attends church regularly and does good deeds seen by others, there is a lot more under the surface that you can't see. There is an inward fear and reverence for God. There is a practice of private devotions.

This important Kingdom Key is essential to experiencing the true fulfillment and power available through God. He requires a humble dependency as we approach Him.

God is the only unfailing and true source for life and He yields His blessings to those who sincerely seek His face above all else.

EMPTY RELIGION

Too many people, like the Pharisees, participate in religion and yet neglect the practices that would yield the true goal and reward of religion - the knowledge of God. These practices include: the cultivation of humility; the practice of regular prayer; the study, meditation and memorization of the Bible; and the private expressions of worship, devotion and love for God.

You see, when we are born again and come alive to God, it is entirely a gift of grace. At the moment we are born again, we receive a new nature because the Spirit of God has joined Himself to our Spirit. Oftentimes this experience is quite overwhelming. Everything seems new. However, the Bible teaches us that we still have our old nature as well.

Having received God's Spirit within, we can and must discipline ourselves to orbit around this new center. This is where the spiritual practices and lifestyle decisions come into play. If you neglect the devotional life, you will find yourself being pulled more and more into the gravitational pull of the old nature.

Your experience of God and your testimony as a Christian largely depend upon the contest between these two natures.

Merely attending church does not by itself decide the issue. If you neglect your private life with God and attend church mainly to see your friends and look good, then you will fall short of the life only God can give you. Each of us must be careful to avoid the trap of using church as merely the center of our social life or as an emotional pit stop to receive an encouraging emotional pick-me-up each week. We must go to church to meet God and let the cross of Christ do its work in us of destroying the old nature so the resurrection life within can be released. And we must have a private devotional life with God throughout the week.

Although many make a show of religion, their neglect of a private devotional life - a secret, hidden life with God, reveals that they are not really seeking God as their source. They have other "idols" in their lives they are serving to receive security, affirmation and identity. These idols could be relationships, a job, children, money, or even church or a ministry. These receive their attention and time. However, none of these will provide true security or fulfillment. By doing this, people nullify the power of true religion.

The Bible clearly declares that many people will fall into this category.

For men will be lovers of self, lovers of money...lovers of pleasure rather than lovers of God, holding to a form of godliness, although they have denied its power...

(2 Timothy 3:2, 4-5)

They have denied the power of religion because they are lovers and seekers of other things over God, falsely believing that happiness, fulfillment or security can be found in them. Society wants to tell us that our happiness and success depend upon our environment, the breaks we get or how others treat us. Do you believe that, or do you believe the Bible that God really is your true source for every good thing?

Faith is blocked when our religious practice is aimed toward impressing others or fitting in. Jesus said to the religious leaders of His time:

How can you believe, when you receive glory from one another and you do not seek the glory that is from the one and only God?

(John 5:44)

Because they practiced their religion looking for affirmation and approval from man, rather than quietly looking to God, they made the growth of faith impossible.

Like the Pharisees, all of us have a deep need for affirmation, approval and love. We might call this "seeking for glory." Unless we first receive these from God in secret, we will be forever grasping after them. We will be driven to gain approval, be complimented and receive credit. We will be controlled by those whose approval we think we need. This will lead to compromise and frustration. However, if we first receive our affirmation, love and approval from God in our private lives with Him, we will be free to live out of the overflow. We will live lives of joyous generosity!

How about you, have you made the discovery of the freedom and joy that come when you begin to live from the inside out instead of the outside in? Whatever the circumstance, look to God first and rest in Him.

People violate this principle when they expect the pastor or church to be their source or supply. Many people are angry at churches or pastors who did not "meet their needs" or fulfill their expectations. Often this is because they were looking to the church or pastor rather than looking to God. Although God uses pastors and other Christians to minister to us, we must not look to them to do what is God's job alone.

When you are in need, do you first turn to the Lord and wait on Him, or do you immediately call the pastor or some other Christian and expect them to carry your problem? God is calling us to become grounded and mature in Him and not dependent upon a pastor as a guru or a church as some form of super-welfare agency. Although a local church body and a pastor are important ways God ministers to us, we must go to Him first and let Him use His servants in our lives as He directs.

We must learn to have a heartfelt trust, dependence and love for God, our heavenly Father. We must rest and trust in His care and provision. A good exercise is to read Psalm 91 where God promises to do twenty-seven things for us if we will do but one — if we will dwell in the shelter of the Most High and abide in the shadow of the Almighty (Psalm 91:1).

STEPS TO DEVELOPING A SPIRITUAL LIFE WITH GOD.

A "spiritual life" or "devotional life" consists of activities that enable people to interact with God in a focused way. These activities are generally in private, involving God and the individual alone. This is where the terms "a hidden life with God" and "a secret history with God" come from. Through the development of this secret, hidden life with God, we come into contact with the very riches and life of God. We encounter resources way beyond what is merely human in order to change ourselves and impact the world around us.

This was the secret of Jesus' life. The Bible tells us He put aside all of His divine attributes and power when He came to earth as a human (Philippians 2:5-8). He lived His life in complete dependence upon God.

He said:

> ...*Truly, truly I say to you, the Son can do nothing of Himself, unless*
> *it is something He sees the Father doing...*
>
> (John 5:19)

The exciting truth of Christian life is we can become like Christ by doing something quite simple...by arranging our lives around the very same activities that Jesus Himself practiced to remain in close, living fellowship with His father. A careful study of Jesus' life reveals that He built His life on a foundation of certain practices: Scripture study, private prayer, simple living, private and public worship, selfless fellowship with others and sacrificial service. All of these practices were carried out to know God better and glorify Him; never to impress others.

The same avenue to God's transforming power, love and grace is available to each one of us. It merely awaits a decision on our part to make a commitment to begin developing a hidden or secret life with God through Jesus Christ.

5

The Kingdom Key to Overcoming Faith

THE PRINCIPLE OF ACTIVE VS. PASSIVE FAITH

For whatever is born of God overcomes the world; and this is the victory that has overcome the world – our faith.

(1 John 5:4)

Everything born of God overcomes the world!

What a wonderful truth!

God is greater than all!

He is greater than anything that would oppose Him or His wise and kind will.

Isn't it wonderful to realize that you and I, as Christians, are born of God as well?

It is our destiny and heritage to overcome!

Notice that faith is the source of our victory. Think of all we have overcome already - death, hell, ignorance of God and hopelessness. Many of us, by coming to Christ, overcame alcoholism, addiction or some other bondage.

Christians are made for victory. Discussing a "Christian living in defeat" is really an oxymoron, a contradiction in terms. However, contradiction or not, many Christians live lives seemingly neither victorious nor successful. They struggle with the same problems over and over again without overcoming them, so there is little joy in their lives.

How is this possible?

One of the most frequent answers is that they do not understand the Kingdom Key to True, Overcoming Faith. This key is *the principle of active faith.* The Bible spells out this principle very clearly in the Book of Romans:

> *That if you confess with your mouth Jesus as Lord, and believe in your heart that God raised Him from the dead, you will be saved; for with the heart a person believes, resulting in righteousness, and with the mouth he confesses, resulting in salvation.*

(Romans 10:9-10)

Verse 10 spells out this necessary key to overcoming faith.

If you ask most Christians why they believe they are going to heaven, they will respond "Because I believe in my heart that Jesus is the Son of God and my Savior." This response reveals a devastating misunderstanding of how faith operates. In fact, it is a misunderstanding that makes overcoming faith impossible.

Read verse 10 again carefully.

It does <u>not</u> state that salvation results from believing. It says that believing results in righteousness which merely gives one access to salvation. It says that salvation itself results from speaking - which is an action.

Understand this important truth: Righteousness, or being in the right, or having the right, is not the same as salvation, or experiencing deliverance and restoration.

To experience God's saving and delivering power in any situation requires that we believe God can and wants to deliver us.

But it requires something more.

It *always* requires that we participate in some faith-inspired action!

If you want deliverance and help from bad habits, depression, unemployment, bad relationships or any other need, you must operate within the principle of *active* faith. In the case of eternal life referred to in Romans 10, the action was confession (probably public confession). In any particular situation where God's saving help is needed, a concrete response or act of faith is needed to manifest the help and power of God.

Although the power and glory belong to God, He requires His people be part of the solution by an exercise of their faith.

TRUE FAITH ALWAYS RESULTS IN DIRECT ACTION

Too many people sit in defeat because they sit in total passivity in their situation, waiting for rescue. Deliverance, however, is delayed, perhaps indefinitely, because they are in violation of this important principle of faith. An obvious and gross example of this, which most of us have seen, is the person who is out of work and says "I am trusting God for a job," and never goes out to look for one.

Is that Bible faith?

Just as foolish is the church that prays for the salvation of the lost, and yet does not have a bold strategy to get out beyond their church walls to reach the lost and then disciple them.

Likewise are parents who pray for God to protect their children from evil and yet fail to do the things that would shield their kids from negative influences, anchor them in the teaching of the Bible or give them a Christian worldview. Can that kind of faith really deliver our children?

Too often we want God to win battles *for* us rather than *through* us. But this misunderstands the purposes of God.

God created mankind to have dominion and rule over all things on earth (Genesis 1:26-28). Although God created the earth, He delegated its rule to mankind. He determined from that point to work through humans on planet earth. God rules directly in heaven, but on earth He rules indirectly through man.

The highest heavens belong to the LORD, but the earth he has given to man.

(Psalm 115:16, NIV)

What is man that You take thought of him, And the son of man that You care for him? You make him to rule over the works of Your hands; You have put all things under his feet.

(Psalm 8:4, 6)

Although God has all power, He has limited Himself to working through humans on earth. For example, whenever God has wanted to communicate to us, He has done it through a human - a prophet or apostle. Even when He wanted to save us from our sins, He did it by becoming one of us. God works through human instruments.

God does His work in partnership with people. This truth is expressed in the following time-tested saying: *Without God we cannot - But without us He will not.*

Faith is the instrument that makes the partnership between heaven and earth and between the divine and human possible. Even Jesus, when He was on earth, did His mighty works by faith.

The Bible teaches that Jesus set aside all His divine power when He became a man (Hebrews 2:5-8). As a result, He did not have the ability to do miracles in Himself but had to walk by faith.

Therefore Jesus answered and was saying to them, "Truly, truly, I say to you, the Son can do nothing of Himself, unless it is something He sees the Father doing..."

(John 5:19)

Jesus came and did the Father's will because He "walked by faith and not by sight" (2 Corinthians 5:7). In so doing, He pleased His Father and overcame every obstacle.

If we are to do the same we must move from merely having faith *in* Jesus to having the faith *of* Jesus. That is, we must move from merely putting our trust in Christ to living as He did and doing what He did. After all, Jesus promised us this.

Truly, truly, I say to you, he who believes in Me, the works that I do, he will do also; and greater works than these he will do; because I go to the Father.

(John 14:12)

Faith is more than trust. It is more than intellectual conviction in the trustworthiness of God. True faith is a conduit between heaven and earth. It allows us a different way of seeing things. As we begin to see a situation as God sees it we become a candidate to be used by God and experience His power.

Faith is seeing what God wants to do in a situation and then acting in such a way as to become His instrument in bringing it about.

Faith is a dynamic force and guide in life. True faith is never passive; it always leads to actions of faith, even if, in some cases, that action might be the obedient decision to do nothing except wait on God's activity or direction for a season. Our faith always gives us direction.

UNDERSTANDING THE WALK OF FAITH

For we walk by faith and not by sight.

(2 Corinthians 5:7)

Our faith requires that we walk and not merely passively sit. "To walk" in the Bible means to live the daily Christian life. The Bible makes this point again and again. Paul said:

The life that I now live in the flesh I live by faith (that is, motivated and empowered by faith).

(Galatians 2:20)

BUT THE RIGHTEOUS man SHALL LIVE BY FAITH (a reference to Habakkuk 2:4).

(Romans 1:17)

Notice that real faith directs and inspires us to action. Real faith must result in action to complete it or release its power.

Faith, if it has no works (or actions), *is dead, being by itself. But are you willing to recognize, you foolish fellow, that faith without works is useless?*

(James 2:17, 20)

Faith, without faith-inspired action, is incomplete and rendered powerless.

It is short-circuited.

While true faith accesses unlimited miracle power, enough to even move mountains (Mark 11:23), a lack of believing and obedient action on our part renders it null and void.

I often see a common example of this principle in some people who tell me they need God's help in their finances. They say they need a miracle. But they refuse to act in that faith to begin to tithe or be faithful in their finances, or give a seed offering. I've pointed out that any miracle God would give them would certainly be able to cover their obedience in this matter. However, their lack of faith-inspired action renders faith incomplete and worthless.

On the other hand, every church is full of people who can testify of the Lord's faithful intervention in their finances when they acted in faith in this matter. I know a couple who have a large family and live on a very modest income. Even so, the wife has a reputation for giving and extreme generosity. God always makes sure their supply is adequate. Amazingly, they enrolled their oldest child in an expensive Christian school - a school that people making much more cannot afford. God has consistently supplied money in a variety of unexpected ways as their lives became an ongoing testimony to the power of true faith.

PASSIVE FAITH IS A CONTRADICTION IN TERMS

If you say you have faith that God can and will do something, it is incomplete or passive faith until you complete it by acting in accordance with that faith. That faith must guide the way you think, speak and act. Are you willing to begin to boldly act in accordance with that belief or conviction? Only then will you begin to see God's wonderful power and deliverance.

Everything God has ever done through our church has involved this principle. We have always had to step out and begin without knowing how everything was going to turn out or how God would supply the new endeavor.

When we felt like God wanted us to start a school we had no teachers, no students, no facility, no money and no experience in starting or running schools. However, we did believe we had the burden and leading of the Lord to do this.

One thing I could do was to travel to Texas and learn from an organization that was running a school. That was the first step. We were stepping out and giving God something to bless. With God's help we kept taking another step, giving God something to bless. Gradually a school was formed. That school has now grown, a high school was added, and now we have 450 students.

Let us again state this important Kingdom Key – the principle of active versus passive faith: Believing in your heart only brings you into the possibility of God's delivering power; it is not until you act in response to faith that it is completed and its reward released.

Sometimes it is hard to know what the response of faith should be. One guideline is to ask yourself, "What would I do if I really felt that what I was believing for was certain?" For instance, if a church really believed God was going to use them to reach the lost, they should start developing plans for making disciples of converts, and for bigger facilities. If a businessman really believed God wanted him to succeed, he should put himself in situations where God could teach him and enlarge him. He should also work hard so God could bless and multiply his efforts.

Perhaps a Sunday school teacher or youth worker is discouraged with their results. Before they simply blame the kids, they must examine their efforts. Are they really expressing faith in their efforts? Are they praying for each child, calling or visiting each child, and preparing each lesson with great care and enthusiasm? Do they have faith that God will use their loving, faith-filled efforts to revolutionize young lives? If not, they are short-circuiting overcoming faith and will not see real victory.

If we want God's blessing, we must give Him something to bless - some effort, endeavor, act of obedience or offering. If we want the fire to fall out of heaven, we must put a sacrifice or offering on the altar (1 Kings 18:38-39; 1 Chronicles 21:26).

God has already taken the initiative by giving us His great promises. Now the ball is in our court; we must act on the basis of the promises and leading of God to see those promises fulfilled.

The real enemy of faith is not so much atheism as a lack of courage and conviction to act on the promises of God regardless of the circumstances. Far more than atheism, this is what hinders God's Kingdom.

How about you? Are you ready to act confidently and boldly on the promises of God? Are you ready to begin to act on the burdens and dreams God has put on your heart and in your spirit? When you accept and act on the principle of active faith you will begin to truly lay hold of the power of God's Kingdom.

6

The Kingdom Key of True Repentance

...if perhaps God may grant them repentance leading to the knowledge of the truth, and they may come to their senses and escape from the snare of the devil...

(2 Timothy 2:25-26)

And when they heard this, they quieted down and glorified God, saying, "Well then, God has granted to the Gentiles also the repentance that leads to life."

(Acts 11:18)

REPENT! The word itself elicits a negative reaction in most people. Perhaps after seeing it you were even tempted to skip this chapter. Most people have a very negative and non-biblical view of repentance. They see it as a very difficult, depressing and negative experience.

While most of us recoil and turn away from any talk of repentance, the Bible reveals a very different picture. As the above verses demonstrate, the Bible reveals that repentance is a precious gift God gives us to lead us to freedom, truth and life.

A right understanding and spirit toward repentance is an important Kingdom Key to unlock the riches of God's Kingdom.

True repentance is a gift from God! It is valuable, precious, and to be prized and sought after. It is a gift that yields incredible blessing and increase.

True and vital repentance yields blessings not possible apart from God. We can only enjoy these blessings as we receive repentance as a gift from God.

Pray this prayer before continuing:

Dear God,
I ask you to illuminate my mind and cause me to understand Your gift of repentance so I may come to embrace a lifestyle of repentance rather than to resist it. May this doorway to Your riches and blessings be opened to me. Amen.

Repentance does not mean depression.

It is positive, not negative.

The Bible teaches that true repentance is "toward God" or a turning to God.

...that they should repent and turn to God...

(Acts 26:20)

REPENTANCE IS POSITIVE

Repentance is a positive turning toward God, the source of truth, life and joy. One of the words translated *repent* is the Greek word *epistrepho* which comes from two Greek words meaning "to turn" and "towards." Of course, repentance also includes a turning away from deception, oppression and death.

Depression does not come from repenting, but from the failure to repent. Heaviness is the spirit of turning away from God, not to Him. Repentance brings an increase to your life, not a subtraction. It expands your personality and freedom, instead of diminishing them, because it adds the blessing of God.

Inevitably, when a person truly repents in some particular area, they experience great joy and victory. On the other hand, people who resist the call of God's Spirit to repent are miserable. Let me share a brief example from my life to illustrate this.

When I was a teenager, in order to finance a surfing trip we wanted to take, some buddies and I decided to sneak into avocado orchards at night and take all the avocados we wanted from several orchards. I justified this to myself by saying "It isn't really stealing. We are just picking avocados off the trees, and nobody will miss them." We sold the avocados and went on our surfing trip.

Let me tell you, I could hardly enjoy myself that whole week! I felt miserable, depressed and cut off from God. It wasn't until I repented much later that I felt the weight of that thievery lift off my spirit and the joy of the Lord return. It wasn't the repentance that made me sad and depressed; it was my resistance to repentance.

Repentance has always been the key offered us to unlock the door into God's superabundant Kingdom. It was the message John the Baptist preached to prepare the way for Jesus who would inaugurate the Kingdom: *"Repent, for the kingdom of heaven is at hand"* (Matthew 3:2).

It was the call Jesus issued to enter His Kingdom: *"The time is fulfilled, and the kingdom of God is at hand; repent and believe in the gospel"* (Mark 1:15).

From that time Jesus began to preach and say, "Repent, for the kingdom of heaven is at hand."

(Matthew 4:17)

We must ask the question: Why is repentance such an indispensable key?

The answer is found in understanding our fallen human nature. Due to the effects of sin and our separation from God, we find our natural self is fatally flawed.

We were created to worship. However, cut off from our Creator, which is our natural focus of worship, we each come to love and worship ourselves. Instead of serving and worshipping God, we have millions of people serving and worshipping themselves. Hence, we have millions of little gods all in conflict with each other.

We were created to live in a dependent and secure relationship with God. However, separated from Him by sin, we find ourselves instead living lives of anxiety, insecurity, envy and fear.

We were created to overcome, not by our own strength, but in virtue of our association and union with God. Separated from Him, however, we find ourselves weak, defeated, enslaved and discouraged. It is clear our human nature is doomed to fail. It is defective and cannot ultimately succeed. It certainly cannot please God with its own righteousness. It does no good to pretend or try to fool ourselves. We won't make any progress in life as long as we are trying to fake it.

Sooner or later, if we are honest, we stop blaming everyone and everything else for our problems, and come to the point of recognizing that we are our own main problem.

However, through repentance we can be delivered from this hopeless situation - repentance is the key.

Through our initial repentance, we come to Jesus as Savior, are born again and receive eternal life.

However, repentance is not just a one-time event, but an ongoing process or lifestyle by which we turn from the brokenness and limitations of our own fractured nature and access the limitless, perfect nature of God.

A lifestyle of repentance is at the heart of the victorious Christian walk. Martin Luther said that true repentance was the daily fleeing from yourself (with your brokenness and limits) to Christ (with His wholeness and power). He termed this "the happy exchange," and so it is. It is a wonderful and joyful thing to exchange your weakness for His strength, your insecurity for His love and assurance, and your ignorance for His wisdom.

Think of every area of your life where you might need God's activity. Now consider this: His wisdom, riches and power will only be available as you turn from self-boasting, self-justifying and self-serving, and turn to Him.

That is called repentance.

Remember, we must not repent only from sin, but also from our self-centered nature and our independence of God.

We must learn to repent of our supposed virtues as well as our vices.

That means we repent of everything we do apart from God - even those things we might justify or even take pride in - if they are flowing from our strength and nature rather than Christ. The Bible calls these "dead works" because they come from our own nature, and lack the life-giving power of God. Sooner or later, all men see the futility of even their best efforts.

> *Therefore leaving the elementary teaching about the Christ, let us press on to maturity, not laying again a foundation of repentance from dead works...*
>
> (Hebrews 6:1)

Repenting from "dead works" is here called a foundation that must be established before we can begin to move into maturity. We cannot grow up into all the promises and callings of God until we make this commitment to repent of our "dead works."

Most people rely upon dead works which cannot truly justify them, satisfy them, deliver them or, in the end, give them eternal salvation. We try to build upon our own good works. We rely on church membership, material possessions, self-help philosophies, popularity or achievements. We concoct arguments to ignore or justify our failings and shortcomings.

However, these are all "dead works" because they have no power to cleanse us from our sins, restore us to the knowledge of God, or give us lasting security, peace, fulfillment or power for living. They cannot make us into the people we truly want to be. Only God can do this. But God can't change us into something we are already pretending to be.

"Dead works" can't give us happiness or real success. In the end they can only lead to disappointment and frustration.

The key to the apostle Paul's amazing life was that he understood this Kingdom principle of repenting from dead works and wrongly-placed confidence.

The apostle Paul had every natural advantage growing up, and had a brilliant mind. Nevertheless, he wrote these words:

> *For we are the true circumcision, who worship in the Spirit of God and glory in Christ Jesus and put no confidence in the flesh... if anyone else has a mind to put confidence in the flesh, I far more. But whatever things were gain to me, those things I have counted as loss for the sake of Christ. More than that, I count all things to be loss in view of the surpassing value of knowing Christ Jesus my Lord, for whom I have suffered the loss of all things, and count them but rubbish so that I may gain Christ, and may be found in Him, not having a righteousness of my own... that I may know Him and the power of His resurrection and the fellowship of His sufferings...*
>
> (Philippians 3:3-4, 7-10)

Paul could have fallen into the trap of leaning and trusting in his many advantages: superior education, natural abilities and well-placed social connections (listed in Philippians 3:4-6). Many people fall into this very same trap today and miss out on fully experiencing the fullness and power of God. Paul, however, made an exciting discovery! He found that if he could turn from self-dependency and pride, he could gain intimacy with Christ and experience His resurrection power. Many people miss out on God's Kingdom and power in their circumstances because they are relying on their own learning, skill, strength or background. I have seen many ministries accomplish little because the ministers were depending upon their education, training or natural leadership skills. Although God will use these things when we surrender them to Him; they, by themselves, are never the source of life or blessings.

Other people never experience the full deliverance that salvation offers because they are trusting in their various coping behaviors such as denial, drugs or alcohol, mood-altering behaviors or compulsions. Rather than boldly coming to Christ in self-abandonment, they continue to cling to their dead works to try to survive. But such things as anger or alcohol or sexual compulsions, or even being consumed with sports or physical fitness, cannot deliver us. Such dead works in the end only result in distracting us and keeping us from experiencing the power and deliverance of God which comes only through repentance.

God has something better for us but we are often afraid to let go of our dead works. Maybe what we have is not that great, but at least it is known and comfortable. To repent means to let go and face the unknown.

Repentance and faith will take you into a better place. Just as our patriarch Abraham found, faith will lead us into a better land with better promises. But just like Abraham, we will have to be willing to leave the familiar and comfortable. We will have to let go of our sinful crutches and dead works to follow God into a land of promise.

Do you believe God has something better for you than what you are now experiencing? Without such a hope you will not embrace repentance. The reason people keep returning to their past and repeating past mistakes is because they don't believe in the future God wants to give them. They don't realize that repentance is a gateway to a better future.

Most people see conviction and repentance as things to avoid instead of gifts from God that need to be embraced. When they experience the initial conviction of the Holy Spirit stirring them to repentance, they want to escape the initial feelings of guilt and the awareness of failure. They, therefore, attempt to escape the conviction of the Holy Spirit by busying themselves with some activity or distraction. Or they perform some token gesture that will quiet the loud promptings of the Holy Spirit in their conscience so they can retreat back to their comfort zones (no matter how dysfunctional or fruitless that comfort zone might be).

Consider the father who, through hearing a sermon or talking to a friend, becomes convicted that he is failing to give enough attention to his kids. The most common thing to do is to try to escape the conviction by making some empty promise to himself or his kids that may never be fulfilled. (For instance, he might say: "As soon as things at work slow down, I am going to take my kids on a camping trip!") Whether this camping trip ever takes place or not, this token gesture is what the man needed to escape conviction. Unfortunately, this father did not resolve the core issue for his children through godly repentance.

When God begins to visit us with the precious gift of conviction which leads to repentance, we should embrace it, stir it up, and give it time to do its full work. God's conviction on that father was meant to revolutionize his relationship with his children. If he had embraced it, a change would have come into his family that would have blessed them tremendously (even the grandchildren and great-grandchildren).

We must change our thinking about conviction and repentance. It is not something to avoid, but something to pray for and embrace. We must not hide from the light. Many people have hidden areas of shame and secret sins in their life. They expend great energy trying to keep these things in the dark. They pretend that they aren't there.

Alcoholics Anonymous has a saying; "You are only as sick as the secrets that you keep." The darkness is not our friend; it is the devil's torture chamber. We must not hide from the light of God's conviction.

When we confess our sins and addictions to God and trusted Christian counselors, we break the hold of darkness and the light can begin to heal and transform us. My friend Jim Newsome likes to say "You can't put something behind you until you face it."

All conviction and repentance lead to overwhelming blessing and enrichment! Isn't it amazing how many of us avoid and fear God's call to grow and change? We will live in great misery and stress rather than simply turn to God and allow Him to change us. Most times, our misery level must reach unbearable limits before we will turn from our pride, fear and "dead works" to turn to God in humble repentance. And then what invariably follows: why, joy, peace and fulfillment.

Being prideful and resistant to the conviction of the Holy Spirit disqualifies one from receiving blessing and growth from God. There are believers today sitting under the finest ministry year after year without any evidence of spiritual growth. Their ears may have heard much biblical truth, but their lives remain unchanged. Ninety-five percent of the time the reason is that they do not embrace conviction and repentance.

Apart from walking in repentance, all the blessings of God remain just out of reach. God calls each one of us to walk in blessing by a humble cooperation with the convictions of His Spirit. The route into the realm of Kingdom life is through a lifestyle of repentance rather than a life of self-serving and self-direction.

In Psalm 32, God calls us to be wise.

I will instruct you and teach you in the way which you should go: I will counsel you with My eye upon you. Do not be as the horse or as the mule which have no understanding, whose trappings include bit and bridle to hold them in check, Otherwise they will not come near to you.

(Psalm 32:8-9)

Many Christians are like that stubborn mule who resists the directions of his master except under the direst of circumstances. In so doing, they miss out on the supernatural Kingdom life. God's conviction must not be taken lightly or resisted lest we become increasingly hard-hearted. Remember, the same sun that softens wax hardens clay.

If we do not respond to the Holy Spirit's prompting, we become hardened to it, and gradually drift from intimacy and union with Christ. Every time we feel the gentle conviction of the Holy Spirit prodding us towards repentance, we have two choices: 1. We can reject what we are hearing and try to escape the conviction through rationalizations and busyness, or 2. We can agree with the whisper of the Holy Spirit and let repentance begin its dynamic and transforming work.

Today, if you hear His voice, do not harden your hearts (see Hebrews 3:7-8).

GOD'S HELP IN REPENTANCE

One of the main reasons Christians run from the conviction of the Holy Spirit is they forget that since God began this work of convicting their heart He will bring it to completion as well. People are afraid that God is going to ask them to do something too hard, and that they will fail.

Thirty years ago, I was a backslidden Christian who resisted any conviction from the Holy Spirit because I was afraid that if I tried to repent and live the Christian life I would fail. Although I was in great misery, I feared God and avoided church at all costs. One evening, because I could not get out of a friend's invitation, I found myself trapped in a church meeting. That night, as the Word of God was shared, the Holy Spirit gave me the gift of repentance. I felt an immediate, overwhelming sensation of joy, peace and release. I was wonderfully set free!

For several days afterwards, I lived in fear that these wonderful new feelings would fade, and that I would go back to my old ways and fail Christ. Then late one evening, as I read my Bible in bed, afraid to go to sleep because I might wake up as the "old me," God taught me a lesson that He burned into my heart. He showed me that He was the Author and

Finisher of true repentance as I read the following words in Philippians and was delivered from my fear of failing as a Christian. I turned off my light and went to sleep.

For I am confident of this very thing, that He who began a good work in you will perfect it until the day of Christ Jesus.

(Philippians 1:6)

That was the secret! Repentance is a work that God not only starts, but energizes all the way to completion! True repentance involves God's partnership and help all the way.

Keep on working with fear and trembling to complete your salvation, because God is always at work in you to make you willing and able to obey His own purpose.

(Philippians 2:12-13, Today's English Version)

...when you received the word of God's message which you heard from us, you accepted it not as the word of men, but for what it really is, the word of God, which also performs its work in you who believe.

(1 Thessalonians 2:13)

What incredible, liberating truths!

What dynamic keys to God's Kingdom!

When God's word of conviction comes to us, it comes with the power to bring effective and lasting repentance! It performs its work in us.

Repentance is the God-given ability to escape our own broken-ness and access God's riches.

This quantum leap can only come from a partnership between our willingness and God's power and ability. True repentance has both a divine and a human side. Always remember: God's call to repentance is also an invitation to share in His riches and glory, and is among the greatest of gifts, to be sought after always. It is a powerful key into the riches of God's Kingdom.

7

The Kingdom Key of Diligence (or Perseverance)

The plans of the diligent lead surely to advantage…

(Proverbs 21:5)

All people have dreams, goals and plans. Many people, however, fail to achieve their dreams and plans. There is one class of person who does not fail or fall short. They are the diligent. Their plans lead surely and certainly to success and advantage. If you have a plan that is pleasing to God and add diligence to it, you will surely move toward success.

LESSONS OF THE CHICK AND THE CATERPILLAR

God has so constructed the universe that it surrenders all its blessings and secrets to those who understand and use the key principles of diligence and perseverance. Since God's purpose is to develop mature sons and daughters, He designed the world so as to require people develop perseverance and patience in order to succeed. He did this by setting into His created order this principle: Nothing worthwhile comes easily. It comes forth only through diligent, patient and sustained effort.

Pat Robertson writes of the reason for this:

Certain risks go with new life and growth - the risks of freedom, we might say - but God prepares us for those risks, through perseverance and struggle, building our muscles, as it were, for each new phase. To refuse to struggle is to stand still, to stagnate.[1]

He then illustrates this principle with a parable from nature, the birth of a baby chick from its egg.

The baby chick, approaching full life, finds himself in a nice, safe environment, dark and quiet. His home, the egg, keeps him warm and cuddly; he feels perfect. Soon, however, he becomes aware that the shell keeping him so comfortable and safe is also circumscribing his life. He begins to feel restricted.

So, the little chick begins pecking at the shell. He doesn't understand it, but things have been set up so that he has to peck and peck and peck. He works very hard, gaining strength hour by hour from that God-ordained struggle. Before long he has attained the strength and endurance to cope with a new environment, and he breaks through the shell.

People have tried to help little chicks by speeding the process, cracking the shell and opening it for them. But, in short-circuiting God's process, they kill the chicks. They are stillborn, unable to handle for even a few moments the rigors of a new environment.[2]

The same principle can be observed with the caterpillar changing into a butterfly. Perhaps you have watched part of the process as a butterfly makes its long, agonizing emergence from the cocoon. Sometimes, people want to help by cutting the cocoon and freeing the butterfly. However, what they find inside the cocoon is a slimy mess. The butterfly is unprepared to emerge and quickly dies.

In the same way, perseverance and diligence are necessary for us if we are to develop and succeed.

Diligence is the consistent, disciplined application of a good strategy until you see success.

Perseverance is the continuing of that effort in the face of hardship or difficulty. The blessings of this world, as well as the mysteries of the Kingdom, open only to the diligent.

> *Poor is he who works with a negligent hand, But the hand of the diligent makes rich.*
>
> (Proverbs 10:4)

> *The hand of the diligent will rule, But the slack hand will be put to forced labor.*
>
> (Proverbs 12:24)

> *For you have need of endurance* (diligent perseverance), *so that when you have done the will of God, you may receive what was promised.*
>
> (Hebrews 10:36)

> *Let us not lose heart in doing good, for in due time we will reap if we do not grow weary* (i.e., stop persevering).
>
> (Galatians 6:9)

"Gotta Have It All Now"

God's important principles of perseverance and diligence fly in the face of our culture's "got to have it all now," instant gratification society. People want and insist on things before they are prepared to use them in a positive and beneficial way. We all know of teens who demanded freedom and independence they were unprepared for, and made decisions that ended up harming their lives.

Unfortunately, this tendency is not limited to teenagers.

Many adults also demand instant success and privilege. They go deep into debt so they can "have it all now," or they take excessive risks in business, wanting to be an overnight phenomenon. They spend money they don't have on lottery tickets and gamble at casinos hoping for a windfall.

The fact of human nature is such that privileges and riches too easily and too soon acquired end up doing more harm than good. The development of diligence and perseverance is an indispensable part of becoming good stewards and life managers.

An inheritance gained hurriedly at the beginning Will not be blessed in the end.

(Proverbs 20:21)

We have all read of people who won money instantly in the lottery or at Las Vegas who had their marriages, friendships and even their lives ruined by the instant wealth and the added responsibilities, opportunities and pressures that came with it. In fact, it is my observation that this is the rule rather than the exception. Consider what happens to many rock stars and athletes who, in our culture, are able to achieve nearly instant celebrity status and wealth. Unprepared for it, they are often destroyed by their quick success.

To prepare people to be successful stewards who handle wealth and power (or any other blessing) correctly, God ordained that things of value would be attained with some difficulty.

Ironically, sitting around dreaming up get-rich-quick schemes is a sure way to wind up poor, but applying yourself diligently will bring a reward.

The soul of the sluggard craves and gets nothing, But the soul of the diligent is made is made fat (or prosperous).

(Proverbs 13:4)

Diligence and perseverance can't be ignored or bypassed. They bring success and increase.

The plans of the diligent lead surely to advantage, But everyone who is hasty comes surely to poverty.

(Proverbs 21:5)

While being diligent leads to advantage, success and prosperity; hastiness or impulsiveness leads to defeat and poverty. People whose lives are marked by impulsive decisions or who are driven by their emotions will disqualify themselves of much happiness and success. They will quit, change or run before the harvest comes. This is the way of God's Kingdom.

THE INCREDIBLE PROMISE OF DILIGENCE

Remember that it is God's good pleasure to share all things with His people. God does not want to withhold any good thing from us. But because He loves us, He wants to protect us by preparing us to handle wisely the good things when they come to us.

He wants His children to grow not only in possessions and blessings but even more in character. This is why God has determined that true blessings only come forth gradually to those who show diligent perseverance in effort and growth. In this way the inward reward of diligence and character come to us as we pursue outward rewards and desires. As we attain diligence, we receive the other rewards.

This makes diligence one of the great secrets of the world.

Diligence has been defined as "a constant, steady effort to achieve."

The key to diligence is consistency and steadiness.

The result of diligence is the development of patience, perseverance and good habits in the pursuit of your goal.

The principle of diligence means that to attain great things does not require heroic effort. Great results and great achievement are achieved by those who employ diligence, that is, a constant and steady effort to achieve.

Popular secular myths even point this out.

For instance, in the story of "The Tortoise and the Hare" (or rabbit), the tortoise challenged the rabbit to a race. Everyone laughed at the tortoise, for turtles are very slow while rabbits are naturally very fast. However, tortoises are known for their determination and the patient pursuit of their destination. During the race, the rabbit took off with a tremendous lead, while the tortoise faithfully plodded along. In time, the quick rabbit found a number of diversions and distractions to occupy him, once even taking a nap. Upon waking from his nap, the rabbit was just in time to watch the slow but diligent tortoise cross the finish line.

I think of this story when I think of a ministry that our church established called "Youth Venture." More than fifteen years ago, a number of us who were troubled about what was happening to the youth of our community were led through prayer to begin an outreach for the youth of our neighborhood. (Chapter Twelve details how the vision for Youth Venture was born). The community our church is in is a troubled one. El Cajon is a city of 95,000 people (it is a suburb of San Diego whose population is over a million). Fifty-one percent of the residences are lower income apartments, most filled with single-parent families. In addition, our city had a national reputation for being one of the methamphetamine production capitals of America. Many of our city's youth were involved in illegal drugs and gangs; our closest high school had a twenty-two percent drop-out rate. In many ways, much of El Cajon was an "inner city" neighborhood, with the racial diversity and problems of an "inner city." What could we, a dozen and a half people from a lower and middle income church of about 350, hope to accomplish? We had very little money and no model to emulate.

Despite all of our shortcomings, God gave us a vision!

We sold Christmas trees and t-shirts, conducted silent auctions and approached Christian businessman for donations. We located a small, 720-square-foot suite and opened a youth game center several blocks from the church in an area with a high population of "at risk" youth. Our all-volunteer staff held regular jobs or attended school, yet we managed to stay open seven days a week. All games and attractions were free; we were there to love the kids.

Within the center we started a Christian club with special events and trips. To become members and participate in these events, the youth would have to go through the one-on-one biblical mentoring program we developed. All the volunteers (including me) committed to doing at least one or two mentoring sessions a week.

It seemed like a small beginning, and at first it started off slow. We all struggled to keep up with the need to mentor. Day in and day out we did one lesson at a time. Each one represented a sacrifice of someone's time. Gradually, the ministry grew and our impact slowly began to be felt.

Today, fifteen years later, we have taken thousands of teenagers through many thousands of lessons. The impact on our community has been substantial as thousands of teens have had the Word of God planted in their hearts in a systematic fashion. Whole families have been won to Christ and our church's own youth ministry has exploded as many of the mentored youth have gone on to be leaders.

That original little youth center of 720 square feet has moved into a new location of 5,000 square feet plus a skate park. In addition we have added three additional teen centers in other neighborhoods. All together our centers occupy 13,000 square feet and average 1,400 visits each week. In addition, we now operate twenty-four afterschool Christian clubs at twenty-four area public schools with hundreds of additional kids involved. Our advisory board now consists of our local congressman, a state assemblyman, a city mayor and a city councilman.

All of this came about simply through daily little actions by the many volunteers that have helped out along the way. Many times I'm sure the volunteers were tempted to wonder if they had really accomplished anything that particular day. And yet, the principle of diligence was quietly at work bringing steady, yet substantial, increase.

The attaining of diligence and perseverance in one's life is greater than the attaining of wealth or power since it alone will determine future success. People who receive great opportunity or advantage, and yet lack diligence, seldom can capitalize on their good fortunes. The opportunity is simply wasted.

A lazy man does not roast his prey, But the precious possession of a man is diligence.

(Proverbs 12:27)

In this scripture, although the lazy man has caught his prey, he lacks the diligence to benefit from the opportunity. It will not become food for him because he will not roast it. For this reason, the man who has diligence, even if he does not presently have his "prey," has a more "precious possession." Opportunities eventually come to all, but only the diligent turn them to their advantage.

Consistency and good habits in the pursuit of our goals are simply essential to success.

Diligence is a guarantee of success for every godly goal. This is surely one of the central truths that come out of Jesus' majestic promise:

Ask, and it will be given to you; seek, and you will find; knock, and it will be opened to you. For everyone who asks receives, and he who seeks finds, and to him who knocks it will be opened.

(Matthew 7:7-8)

Many people have unnecessarily struggled with this verse. They wonder how it can be taken literally. It is a mystery to them because they do not fully grasp the Kingdom Key of Diligence. As has been pointed out in countless sermons and Bible studies, the verbs "ask," "seek" and "knock" are all Greek present tense imperatives, giving them the literal meaning "keep asking" and it shall be given to you; "keep seeking" and you shall find; "keep knocking" and it shall be opened to you.

What Jesus is doing here is assuring us of God's willingness to give us all good things, and He is underscoring the power of the Kingdom Key of Diligence.

Jesus does not place limitations on the size of the goal you may be seeking; there is no limit on what God can accomplish when His power is linked to a person or group that understands and practices the Key of Diligence. He simply says, "Ask, seek and knock." Much of our failure is because we simply quit; we grow discouraged by obstacles and delays and listen to the voice of the enemy who says "You're not going to make it," "You are not accomplishing anything," "It must not be God's will for you to reach this goal," etc.

The truth is that it probably *is* God's will, and the obstacles and delays are simply there to build stamina and character to prepare us to receive it. God is bringing us down the road to growth and success. However if we quit, then we fail.

THE SECRET OF DILIGENCE

The secret of diligence is to realize that God supplies everything we need to succeed in those dreams and desires He puts in our hearts. The problem comes when we do not diligently persevere in following the direction God has given us.

Hebrews 2:1 is instructive in this regard. The writer is addressing those who, through lack of diligence in studying gospel truths, were in danger of backsliding into some legalistic Jewish practices and beliefs.

> *For this reason we must pay much closer attention to what we have heard, so that we do not drift away from it.*
>
> (Hebrews 2:1)

Although they had been taught the glorious gospel truths that lead to freedom and fullness, through a lack of diligent study and practice they were becoming confused and compromised. They were letting their gospel truths slip away.

We can lose anything God shows us or gives us in the Spirit through a lack of diligence. Many times, when God gives us an insight or some direction for our lives, rather than meditating upon it or practicing it until we are established in it, we are careless and unfruitful with it and let it slip away.

Think of how much you may have already missed as result of not being faithful with truths or direction that God gave you.

Many people have responded many times to a sermon or a word God gave them by making a vow or decision, and then simply let the vow slip away from them through a lack of diligence. A part of diligence is holding on to things that God has given you by putting them into practice until they bring their blessing and increase. One of the saddest things for me as a pastor is to watch people who are getting glorious deliverances and spiritual breakthroughs, and who through laziness and lack of continuing in the Word and fellowship, fall back into their old bondages.

In 2 Peter 1:10-11 we are assured that as long as we diligently practice the things we have been given and taught, we will never stumble, and the entrance to His Kingdom will be abundantly supplied.

Therefore, brethren, be all the more diligent to make certain about His calling and choosing you; for as long as you practice these things, you will never stumble; for in this way the entrance into the eternal kingdom of our Lord and Savior Jesus Christ will be abundantly supplied to you.

(2 Peter 1:10-11)

The principle of diligence should be a tremendous encouragement to every Christian. In my own life, this one principle has been a constant source of encouragement to me. It assures me that even though I am no superman, I can still accomplish great things and have an impact on my world. I may not be capable of heroic or superhuman effort, but I can be diligent and see the increase build.

Remember, the key to lasting victory and success is not the hugeness or greatness of the initial effort, but the commitment to constant, steady effort and growth.

Our church, Foothills Christian Church, is a testimony to the power of this Kingdom Key. When we first began, there was nothing to suggest that it would succeed. It had no affiliation, backing or advantage. Its leadership core had no superior talent or gifting, and little experience.

For the first three years, our church struggled. Many involved were tempted to quit (some did). However, each year we grew in experience and opportunities. Diligence paid off in greater and greater accomplishments and victories. Each one built on the last.

DILIGENCE AND THE SPIRITUAL LIFE

Diligence is a key in every effort, even our walk with God. God Himself is a rewarder of diligence.

> *But without faith it is impossible to please him: for he that cometh to God must believe that he is, and that he is a rewarder of them that diligently seek him.*

> (Hebrews 11:6, KJV)

To be diligent in seeking God does not require that we become monks, or even that we have great amounts of discretionary time for burdensome fasts or pilgrimages. It means that we begin to sanctify some portion of our daily and weekly life as set apart for regular and sustained spiritual growth. For some, it may simply mean fifteen minutes of prayer a day, thirty minutes of Bible study three times a week, and attending church and home fellowship once a week, for example.

Remember, the secret is not the size of the chunk of time, but the consistency and faithfulness over time. Diligence means that we are serious about a schedule and do not alter it every time it involves some small inconvenience. Such a schedule, diligently followed, when combined with true humility and obedience, will produce spiritual growth.

Too many Christians miss out on the blessing and guidance God has for them because they are not diligent. Christians miss out on appointments with God because, through a lack of diligence, they are not where they should be at the right time.

Every pastor and Bible teacher knows the following equation to be true, based on experience and observation: The likelihood of a person missing a service or Bible study is in direct proportion to that teaching being of direct relevance to their life.

As a young pastor, I often noticed a definite phenomenon. When I had a message I knew was important for someone to hear, that person would almost invariably not be at the meeting! I marveled at this, and at first thought it must just be a coincidence or a product of my imagination. However, eventually I had to admit it was a real phenomenon.

There was one exception to this rule.

Those people who never missed attending, unless they were very sick or had some legitimate emergency (those who were diligent), always seemed to be there when the word was especially meant for them.

One day I realized the reason for this. When a word from God (the most precious thing in the world) was waiting for someone, Satan, the enemy of our soul, would put up some small inconvenience or distraction to discourage that person from attending. God would allow this small obstacle, no doubt, to test the person to see if he or she would be found faithful and diligent.

Unfortunately, many failed this test and left themselves thereby disadvantaged. As a result of this insight, I formulated the following principle:

Only the diligent hear the word of God.

DILIGENCE GIVES US GREAT REWARD IN THE SPIRITUAL LIFE

Consider the following: While many people struggle and know little of the rest that God provides, the diligent enter into that rest.

> *For the one who has entered His rest has himself also rested from his works, as God did from His. Let us therefore be diligent to enter that rest...*
>
> (Hebrews 4:10-11)

People who are diligent in prayer, Bible study, obedience, fellowship and seeking after God experience a rest in God that nothing can shake them out of.

While many people struggle with doubt and despair, the diligent have the key to unshakable confidence and hope and always receive the promise.

> *And we desire that each one of you show the same diligence so as to realize the full assurance of hope until the end, so that you will not be sluggish, but imitators of those who through faith and patience inherit the promises.*
>
> (Hebrews 6:11-12)

While many people struggle with feeling ashamed before God, diligence allows us to receive the witness that we are approved of God.

> *Be diligent to present yourself approved to God as a workman who does not need to be ashamed, accurately handling the word of truth.*
>
> (2 Timothy 2:15)

If we understand the principle of diligence and perseverance, we have an important key to understand how the world operates, and a powerful tool that will open the door to success and achievement. Just as bountiful crops are the result of regular, gentle rains, so most blessing and growth come as a result of consistent, faithful obedience. Many people, after an experience with God, expend all their energies in a relatively short burst of great activity, and then burn out or drop out before they see their hopes realized.

This is the mistake many people make when they begin some new undertaking, such as a new job, business or ministry, with great enthusiasm. After a great outburst of effort, they drop out, disappointed and sometimes bitter, because their naive "instant success" dreams were not realized.

Great harvests do not come from flashfloods or sudden, torrential rains. These usually produce destruction rather than growth.

It is the same way with suddenly and explosively expending all our efforts at once - it usually creates more upheaval and confusion than growth. We fail because we ignore the powerful requirement and dynamic of diligence. Success in all areas of life requires time, patience, perseverance and diligence. The exciting news is that these will bring about success for every godly goal in your heart.

Every individual can know success in every area of life if they apply the dynamics of this truth.

8

The Kingdom Key of Reciprocal Returns: Understanding the Law of Sowing and Reaping

Do not be deceived, God is not mocked; for whatever a man sows, this he will also reap.

(Galatians 6:7)

The Law of Reciprocal Returns, also known as the Law of Sowing and Reaping, is a powerful dynamic shaping and affecting the life of every individual alive today. It is a powerful principle that affects us every day of our lives.

As I have counseled, listened to and talked with thousands of people over the years, I have come to see the Law of Sowing and Reaping is at the very core of how life works. No other single factor affects the present and future circumstances of an individual as much this law.

We first see this law spoken into existence on the third day of Creation.

Then God said, "Let the earth sprout vegetation, plants yielding seed, and fruit trees on the earth bearing fruit after their kind with seed in them"; and it was so.

(Genesis 1:11)

Here we see that God created the original plants and trees but He then gave them the ability to produce seed that would bring forth still other plants and trees.

Likewise, in creating all living creatures, He decreed that they would produce "after their kind." God gave the Creation an expanding potential - an ability to multiply and bring forth increase. This fruitfulness is built into the fabric of the world. We have been given the power to bring forth new life, increase and prosperity!

However, on that day, God instituted a law to limit this ability to multiply and increase. Everything would produce or multiply only "after its own kind." Our ability to create is subject to this law.

We have the ability to bring forth new life. We can, God willing, bring forth a family. However, it will be a family of humans, not water buffaloes.

We can produce food. We can grow a garden or raise a herd. However, if we want corn, we had better have seeds for corn. No other seed we plant will give us corn.

Each seed can only produce a crop after its own kind. Everyone over the age of three understands this principle. What many do not understand is that this principle works in every area of God's Creation, not just agriculture and biology, but every area of life.

A UNIVERSAL LAW

When we look at other areas of life, however, it seems that many people feel that this basic Creation principle can be ignored. They believe they can be an exception to this law. They hope to create good results for themselves through unrighteous actions or deceit. They are seemingly unaware that evil can only produce more evil.

Generation after generation of foolish and naive people make shipwrecks of their lives trying to disprove this law.

They are deceived.

Jesus taught and lived by this Kingdom principle. For example, He stopped His followers from taking up the sword by saying:

…Put your sword back into its place; for all those who take up the sword shall perish by the sword.

(Matthew 26:52)

Jesus understood that violence could only beget more violence. He knew that His Kingdom of peace could only come by planting seeds of peace. Violence must beget more violence. It can only produce after its own kind.

In the same way, love will produce more love. It is the law of the universe.

In physics, we know that for every action there must be an equal and opposite reaction; there will be a predictable and corresponding result for every action. This is why, for instance, we can predict the movement of a jet plane in the sky. We can plot the speed and direction of that jet if we know the thrust and direction of the air exiting the turbines, and take into account other natural laws like friction and gravity.

This is also true in the spiritual realm, which is part of the same Creation made by the Creator who is consistent in His laws. By knowing God's Word we can reliably predict the future outcome of our actions

Note how Jesus taught that this Kingdom Key of Reciprocal Returns works when He said,

Be merciful, just as your Father is merciful. Do not judge, and you will not be judged; and do not condemn, and you will not be condemned; pardon and you will be pardoned. Give, and it will be given to you…

(Luke 6:36-38)

Here we are given the secret to a successful and fulfilling life!

Give and it shall be given back to you. For every action there will be a predictable and corresponding reaction.

There it is.

A golden key to success.

We need not be subject to circumstances or the wrong actions of others. We are to *act* in faith rather than *react* to circumstances or the actions of others, and we will see a blessing released into our life.

One caution must be added. Just as in the illustration of the jet plane, which had to take into account all relevant laws like gravity and friction, we must likewise remember that other spiritual laws may affect the outcome of our sowing and reaping. In addition, remember, God is not a machine. Such things as the motives of our heart and our relationship to God certainly have a profound effect on the outcomes of our actions. Life is ruled over by a sovereign God.

BREAKING THE CHAIN

Jesus taught His disciples in regard to this important principle. He taught them not to react in kind to the bad actions of others toward them. They were not to continue the chain of producing evil, but were to overcome evil by acting in an opposite way, thereby releasing the seed for a good return.

> *But I say to you who hear, love your enemies, do good to those who hate you, bless those who curse you, pray for those who mistreat you. Whoever hits you on the cheek, offer him the other also; and whoever takes away your coat, do not withhold your shirt from him either. Give to everyone who asks of you, and whoever takes away what is yours, do not demand it back. Treat others the same way you want them to treat you.*
>
> (Luke 6:27-31)

Here Jesus shows us that we can write our prescription for life. Regardless of how others treat us, we should treat them in the way that we want to be treated. When you simply react to the actions of others, you are letting them determine what type of seeds you will plant and therefore what your future harvest will be. If you want the blessings of the Kingdom than *you* must choose what seeds you will plant. Don't let someone else determine what you future harvest will be.

We must *act- not react.* Soon, we will find that through the Law of Reciprocal Returns others are beginning to treat us in the same way.

Give a smile, get a smile.

Give respect, get respect.

Act like a friend and you will find friends all over. Treat enemies like friends and soon you will find they are friends.

PLANNING A HARVEST

Look again at the verse that began our study. It makes it clear that this law, also known as the Law of Sowing and Reaping, is not limited to agriculture.

> *Do not be deceived, God is not mocked; for whatever a man sows, this he will also reap. For the one who sows to his own flesh will from the flesh reap corruption, but the one who sows to the Spirit will from the Spirit reap eternal life.*
>
> (Galatians 6:7-8)

Do not live under the deception that the Creator's law can be ignored. People do so to their own misery and destruction. People who sow ungodly and unspiritual seeds of lust, greed, anger, pride and selfishness can only reap a future harvest of diminishment and unhappiness.

But this principle is also a liberating and powerful truth for our good. It is the key our Creator gave us to empower us to have happiness and success. It means we can achieve our desires for growth, happiness and godly prosperity. If we will simply select the right seeds and plant them we can receive a wonderful harvest.

Contrary to what some people think, faith is more than asking God for what you need but don't have. That is merely a request. Faith is releasing something you have in expectation of a multiplied return. Faith means planting seeds because you believe in the Lord of the Harvest and His promises.

Even if you don't think you have much, you have something. It might be ten dollars, or one night a week, or the gift of friendship. Whatever it is, plant it - invest it somewhere because you believe God will reward you with a return. The seed for the harvest that you will need tomorrow is in your hand today. Ask yourself; "What is in my hand? What do I have to invest?"

A DANGEROUS LIE

Our culture has embraced a worldview of victimization. Many people largely understand themselves or others as victims. Our society has many people who feel helpless and trapped, unable to change or control their lives. We look for people or circumstances to blame: parents, racism, poverty, siblings, the system, etc.

Entire mega-industries have grown up around the concept that people are victims. We feel our lives have been determined by other persons, and by events beyond our control.

Certainly we cannot ignore that others have had the opportunity to profoundly affect our lives for good or ill. But an understanding of this Kingdom Key shows that we are not passive victims of life.

We have the God-given power to determine our life!

No matter what our previous circumstances or experiences, we can begin to create our future today.

All of us have the ability to begin to sow seeds. We all have the ability to determine a future harvest by the careful selection of the right seeds today.

Seeds we sow can be words, attitudes, actions or resources. Because we live in an orderly, law-obeying creation, our harvest will be a reflection of the seeds we plant, irrespective of who we are or what our background was. Good seeds are those thoughts, acts and words that are in keeping with God's revealed Truth in the Bible.

People waste much time and energy blaming others or their bad luck for conditions in their lives. In doing so, they may gain a false comfort but they are also defining themselves as victims rather than victors and can therefore only expect more of the same in the future.

People reap what they sow, whether they are willing to recognize it or not. Their lives are largely a result of the words, attitudes and actions they sow. While this might at first seem like a bitter pill to swallow, it opens the door to a hope-filled future.

THE DYNAMICS OF HARVEST

To fully grasp this powerful principle and make it work for you, you must understand several simple truths associated with it.

You always harvest in a different season than you plant.

There is a growing season in which the farmer must wait before he can get the harvest. Sometimes, he must continue to irrigate or pull weeds in the garden during this period. For much of the time, the growth is under the surface, invisible to his observation.

The same is true for living organisms that grow inside of their mother or inside an egg for the first months of life. It's only by faith that we know growth is taking place, even though we cannot see it.

This truth relates to growing and harvesting in other areas of life as well. In the early period of the process, there may be nothing encouraging in sight. Nevertheless, the harvest is growing.

We must believe in God's laws. We must not go and dig up the seed or give up and move away from the garden that we have planted.

We must have faith and be patient!

The Bible tells us in the very next verse:

Let us not lose heart in doing good, for in due time we will reap if we do not grow weary.

(Galatians 6:9)

For instance, if someone has been sowing seeds of criticism or discord in their marriage for months or even years, they cannot expect everything to change because of one kind act. They must continue to plant good seeds and be patient; soon the harvest of the good seeds will overtake and overwhelm the harvest of the bad seeds that were planted.

The same is true in the area of finances. If you have been having financial problems and decide to start tithing on Sunday and you receive a financial blessing on Monday — that isn't sowing and reaping — that is a miracle. It is a gracious gift of God to encourage you. Thank God for your miracle, but you still need to establish the habit of sowing good seed (which includes giving tithes and offerings) for your future harvest or you will continue to have financial difficulties. We cannot presume to live by miracles but by reaping the good seeds we plant.

In any area that you are struggling, begin to plant good seeds. The harvest will come, but it does require patience.

...The farmer waits for the precious produce of the soil, being patient about it, until it gets the early and late rains. You too be patient; strengthen your hearts...

(James 5:7-8)

If a farmer were to grow discouraged and impatient because of the length of the growing season and abandon his field, he would miss out on gaining the harvest. He must be patient and wait for things that are beyond his control, like the coming of the rains. So, too, we must be patient and believing and let God bring the harvest.

In the early stages of the growing season, the crop may not resemble what we expect.

God showed me this one day when, as a young man, I was very discouraged (I was frequently discouraged in those days when I did not see the results for which I was hoping). One day as I read Scripture and prayed over a situation that I had put much faith and work into, and yet which looked very discouraging, these words of Jesus seemed to leap off the page at me.

...The kingdom of God is like a man who casts seed upon the soil; and he goes to bed at night and gets up by day, and the seed sprouts up and grows - how, he himself does not know. The soil produces crops by itself; first the blade, then the head, then the mature grain in the head. But when the crop permits, he immediately puts in the sickle, because the harvest has come.

(Mark 4:26-29)

That day this passage hit my mind like an explosive bolt of lightning. I realized several critical things.

Every seed planted will grow whether or not the growth process is understood by the one planting the seeds.

Seeds planted in soil sprout up and grow even though most people do not understand the process. Jesus said it was the same with the Kingdom.

The laws and operations of the Kingdom would operate and bring forth increase from the good seeds I planted, even if I didn't understand how. One day, the crop would be ready, and I could reap the harvest.

The early stages of the crop do not look like the harvest.

The early stages of a crop do not look like what you hope for unless you are trained or educated to recognize it. The crop would come up first as a blade, then the head, and only then the mature grain in the head.

Imagine someone not familiar with farming wanting to grow corn. After they plant corn seeds, they irrigate and patiently wait for the harvest. One day, little sprouts begin to come up. "Oh no," they think, "What is this? What happened to the beautiful corn I was waiting for?"

The early stages of corn do not look like the great, tall stalks full of rich, yellow corn that come later.

When I was a little boy I planted a vegetable garden. When some of the sprouts came up, I pulled them out because to me they looked like grass or weeds. In the same way, in the early stages, the fruit of our faith, prayers and efforts may not look at all like the mature, finished product. We may even curse them and be tempted to pull them up.

This principle has been very true in my life. Many events and relationships that at one time I judged as failures or defeats have developed, in the timing of God, into very great blessings in my life.

If you are patient, you will find the same to be true in your own life. If you plant good seeds, eventually God will bring forth a good harvest, despite how things look now.

You will always harvest more than you sow.

Things multiply.

If you plant a tiny seed of corn, eventually you will not only get a huge stalk of corn, but that stalk will contain many more seeds of corn. In the same way, opportunities for growth and success multiply. Most Christians understand that God is their source of supply. At mealtimes they give thanks over their food, realizing that God supplied it. When they receive a raise or a promotion, they thank God, realizing that *"Every good thing given and every perfect gift is from above, coming down from the Father of lights..."* (James 1:17). They realize that God supplies us.

Far fewer, however, realize that God not only supplies - *He multiplies.* Paul expounds on this powerful truth in his second letter to the Corinthians.

Now He who supplies seed to the sower and bread for food will supply and multiply your seed for sowing and increase the harvest of your righteousness; you will be enriched in everything for all liberality...

(2 Corinthians 9:10)

Look carefully at the above verse. We see that God supplies two things. He supplies bread for food, but He also supplies something more glorious, He supplies seed for sowing. Most Christians pray for their daily bread or daily needs. We pray and thank God at mealtimes for the food we are about to consume. We are grateful that God is faithful to supply our needs.

But God gives us something far greater. He supplies us all with seed for sowing. Seed is different from bread. Seed is greater than bread. The blessing and increase and miracle are not in the bread which is eaten but in the seed which is sown.

Bread is eaten and it is gone. But seed is sown and it multiplies. Some people trust God only for bread. Others do that but also believe God for seed.

The potential for multiplication is only in that which you sow (give away). Everyone who wants to experience Kingdom multiplication must move from being a taker to being a giver - from just being an eater to being a sower.

Open up your wallet. How much money is in it? Can you tell which of it is bread and which of it is seed? Bread and seed look identical in your wallet. It's up to you to prayerfully decide how much of it is seed. But, be sure of this, no matter how little you have, some of it is seed because God's Word says that He supplies you with both.

If you just want a temporary full stomach, eat it all. If you want to see a multiplied harvest, call some of it seed and sow it. This is true for money, time, energy and love. Don't tell me what you need or what you don't have. Tell me what you have and what you are willing to call seed and then sow it.

Few other Laws of the Kingdom will exercise such a profound impact on your life as this one. By consistently planting good seeds you will change your life and world.

9

The Kingdom Key of Giving

As we have seen, the principle of reciprocal returns shows that the secret to success and happiness lies in giving, not taking.

Giving is foundational to benefiting from the riches and supply of God's Kingdom. You give your love, forgiveness, time and material goods. Over time, it will all return to you many times over. Giving, not receiving holds the potential for Kingdom multiplication. No wonder Paul quotes Jesus as saying:

> ...and remember the words of the Lord Jesus, that He Himself said, "It is more blessed to give than to receive."
>
> (Acts 20:35)

Through the dynamics of the Kingdom, the blessing or true increase lies in the giving, not the receiving. We must learn to be givers. We cannot be selfish givers; giving in hope of our own benefit...we must give in love, as we are prompted by the Holy Spirit. None of us are natural-born givers. We are all born as takers. But giving is a skill and a freedom we can all learn through God's grace.

Although giving cuts across our natural inclination to grasp and hoard out of fear and greed, it is a key to God's Kingdom that will unleash blessing and increase. Like all of the Kingdom principles, it seems upside down to our natural thinking and instincts (remember God's ways are not like our ways).

Becoming truly generous givers is the path to blessing and prosperity.

He who is generous will be blessed...

(Proverbs 22:9)

There is one who scatters (that is gives away generously), *and yet increases all the more, And there is one who withholds what is justly due, and yet it results only in want.*

(Proverbs 11:24)

The generous man will be prosperous, And he who waters will himself be watered.

(Proverbs 11:25)

People who are in financial difficulties must learn this principle. Poor people, just as much as the rich, must learn how to give. Over time, it will change their lives.

If you are in financial difficulty, or any other difficulty, you must begin to give...give money, time and compassion. Give obediently and sacrificially as you feel the Lord directing you.

Ask God to help you develop a generous heart. Learn to give joyfully and freely. Don't fall into the trap of giving in a self-seeking or calculated way. Just let it go out joyfully just as Jesus directed us *"...Freely you received, freely give"* (Matthew 10:8) and *"...do good, and lend, expecting nothing in return* (Luke 6:35). Give joyously knowing that God will be faithful to you as you are generous. Generosity doesn't give to receive - but generosity is always rewarded by God. The secret to entering in to God's economy of blessing is to give freely, entrusting your reward entirely to God alone.

All these blessings will come upon you and overtake you, if you obey the LORD your God.

(Deuteronomy 28:2)

You must stay focused on loving and serving Jesus and simply let the blessings "come upon you and overtake you" at Jesus' direction. Believe me; they will come from surprising places in surprising ways.

Once we were approached by a woman who had just received temporary custody for her thirteen-year-old nephew while his parents were in jail. She approached us at Youth Venture for help. We gave much time and effort to her nephew over the next two years while she had custody. We saw very encouraging results in the boy. About a month after he was returned to his parents we received a $50,000 check to Youth Venture from a man we had never heard of. It was and is the largest single contribution Youth Venture has ever received. It turns out that the woman who approached us about the boy worked as a secretary for him. He was looking for a place to give and had observed our efforts with the boy from afar. Over the next two years we received an additional $60,000 from him. As we gave freely, God had sent a great blessing to overtake us.

This Kingdom principle is not meant to serve our greed but to release us from the fear of giving.

God, your Father, does not want you worried about finances. Jesus was not worried about money and finances. He did not serve money, nor was He a slave to His circumstances. He knew how to walk in His Father's supply. God wants you to be free both from the love of money and from the fear of not having enough.

> *And God is able to make all grace abound to you, so that always having all sufficiency in everything, you may have an abundance for every good deed.*
>
> (2 Corinthians 9:8)

> *...and my God will supply all your needs according to His riches in glory in Christ Jesus.*
>
> (Philippians 4:19)

Jesus said that we are to be no more burdened by financial concerns than the birds of the air or the flowers of the field (Luke 12:22-31).

A PERSONAL EXAMPLE

When I was twenty-seven, I felt strongly led to leave the mainline seminary I had been attending for two years. In my mind, they had moved away from the gospel. This decision to leave meant losing what little financial support I had been receiving. To make it even harder, the day after I made the decision I discovered that my wife, Linda, was pregnant with our first child.

We returned to San Diego penniless and with my wife four months pregnant. We both found summer jobs, and we rented a single room in a large house. Even though it was hard, God had already taught us His principle about sowing and reaping, so we were unafraid.

As the new school year began in my new seminary, I had to quit my fulltime summer job to work part time and finish up seminary here in San Diego. Linda soon had to quit her job to tend to our new baby. We knew that the only way we could make it financially would be to tap into Kingdom economics.

That meant giving.

I needed a part-time job, but instead of looking for the highest paying one available, I looked for a ministry position where I could give. I took a part-time position at a church as youth pastor.

The pay was only $600 a month, but it gave me the opportunity to give of myself and my gifts. Linda and I gave ourselves - heart and soul - to that work. The first month we were there, over $500 in anonymous donations came in to us!

It never stopped!

We gave money away at every opportunity we had. At the beginning, when an opportunity to give money would come up and I would tell Linda that we should give generously, she would look at me, puzzled, and say, "You are not serious! How can we possibly afford to give away money right now?"

My response to her would always be exactly the same. I would say, "How can we afford not to give? We can't possibly afford to live on our income. We must tap into the Lord's economy."

The Lord continued to return to us several fold in many different ways. After the birth of our first son, Neil, we received an opportunity for extremely low-cost housing. When our second child, Brice, was born, we received free housing (paying only for utilities).

Many times money would come to us mysteriously.

One time I was praying about a financial need and I felt led to open up my Bible to read. I opened it up to discover $300 in twenties someone had apparently stuck in there. Another time, Linda was praying about a financial need when she felt led to run up and check the mailbox. In it was an envelope with $200 in it, and a short note from an anonymous person saying that God had impressed them to give it while in prayer.

Many times, and in many ways other than financial, God multiplied back to us what we gave. I was at that church for two and one-half years and the salary never went above $1,000 per month. Nevertheless, we gave a higher percentage of our money away (after the tithe was paid) than at any other time of our lives.

We never did without.

God always met every need.

The board at Foothills Christian Church operates with the same understanding. We have always tried to be a church that gives generously. We have many times given sacrificially to other churches. When we were trying to build our first church building, due to additional requirements by the municipal authorities, we had significant cost overruns. We needed to raise about $30,000 more to finish the job. We were a small and poor church. We did not have any idea where that money would come from.

It was a very serious problem.

The job was more than half over, and we had a four-year lease to honor. We felt like everything was on the line.

We did serious praying.

At that same time, we heard about a pastor friend of ours who had just rented space for his church which was even smaller than ours. He needed $3,000 to buy chairs and make various improvements to be able to move in and use it.

We saw this as the Lord's answer to us, and we immediately decided to give that church some money. At the board meeting, Dave (my brother and co-pastor) and I reported the need, and suggested we give that church one or two thousand dollars.

The board insisted we give the entire $3,000! This amount represented a very large percentage of what we had left to continue work on our building. But, as a result of that giving, in a most remarkable fashion, God moved on other hearts to meet our entire need for $30,000 as well.

The old saying is certainly true: "You cannot out-give God."

Understanding how the principle of sowing and reaping operates within the Kingdom Key of Giving has helped us expand as a church ministry. For instance, some years ago we heard of a church in inner city Los Angeles called the L.A. Dream Center, pastored by Tommy and Matthew Barnett. This church had a tremendous ministry to the people of their community. They needed to raise a very large sum of money to pay for an abandoned hospital they were trying to buy. Once again, we were trying to raise money for an expansion project of our own.

I realized that the L.A. Dream Center was already doing many of the things that we dreamed of doing in our community, and in a much poorer area. I knew that if we wanted God to supply our dream to reach the people of our community, we must first be willing to invest in the ministry of someone else who was already doing many of those very same things.

As before, we went to the church board. Once again, they suggested a higher number than the one we initially suggested. Although we already gave a large amount to missions each month, we as a board voted to send $15,000 out of our building fund to the L.A. Dream Center.

About one year later, I was praying about how to finance and increase Youth Venture, our outreach ministry to the youth of our community. It was growing, but it had to compete with other ministries at our church for money.

Several days later, on December 22 of that year, two businessmen who did not attend our church and were unknown to each other came in within thirty minutes of each other and gave checks totaling $54,000. These gifts were completely unexpected and totaled nearly twice the budget for Youth Venture the previous year.

I believe these events represent the operation of the principle of giving in action. Learning to give joyously and generously is a key that opens the bank of heaven and leads one into an adventure of God's blessing and increase.

THE TEN PERCENT SOLUTION

One more thing must be said...you can only give what is yours. You cannot give what belongs to another. In the financial realm, the first ten percent of our income belongs to God. This is the tithe; tithe means "a tenth." The Bible is very clear that everything belongs to God.

The earth is the LORD'S, and all it contains, The world, and those who dwell in it.

(Psalm 24:1)

"The silver is Mine and the gold is Mine," declares the LORD of hosts.
(Haggai 2:8)

As landlord and owner, God requires that we pay back one tenth of our increase with a grateful heart for the furtherance of His Kingdom on earth.

This is a requirement, not an option!

...all the tithe of the land... is the LORD'S; it is holy to the LORD.
(Leviticus 27:30)

"Tithe" simply means "a tenth." The tithe is a tax God as owner places on everything. It is not a gift. That is why the Bible never speaks of "giving" a tithe, but rather of "paying" the tithe. We "give" offerings but we "pay" tithes. Since the tithe belongs to God, He calls those who do not pay it "thieves and robbers." Here is how God spoke through the prophet Malachi:

"Will a man rob God? Yet you are robbing Me! But you say, 'How have we robbed You?' In tithes and offerings. You are cursed with a curse, for you are robbing Me, the whole nation of you! Bring the whole tithe into the storehouse, so that there may be food in My house (for the priests), *and test Me now in this," says the LORD of hosts, "if I will not open for you the windows of heaven, and pour out for you a blessing until it overflows. Then I will rebuke the devourer for you..."*
(Malachi 3:8-11)

This scripture points out that paying the tithe does two things. First, it opens the windows of heaven so that a heavenly blessing can be poured out upon us, and secondly it prompts God to rebuke the devourer from our finances. Robbing God of His tithe will keep the windows of heaven closed and release the devourer into your finances.

Understanding the Principal of Sowing and Reaping, we must ask ourselves, "How can prosperity or happiness come from stealing from God?"

Only evil can come from evil.

We will put ourselves under a financial curse rather than a blessing. It is the Law of the Universe. The "devourer" will devour our blessings. We will be like the other people who tried to steal from God.

Now therefore, thus says the LORD of hosts, "Consider your ways! You have sown much, but harvest little; you eat, but there is not enough to be satisfied; you drink, but there is not enough to become drunk, you put on clothing, but no one is warm enough; and he who earns, earns wages to put into a purse with holes."

(Haggai 1:5-6)

We must not be like the children of the world who are ignorant and live in darkness. We must live as children of God who prosper by understanding God's laws. People who do not believe in or understand the Kingdom of God feel that it would be "impossible" to tithe. This is because they have not discovered how obedience to God's Kingdom principles opens up "the windows of heaven" for blessing and increase. Millions of Christians can give testimony to how tithing and giving to God's Kingdom has brought increase into their lives. Jesus truly is Lord...even over finances.

Let me ask you what appears to be a simple question, "Which is more, ninety percent or one hundred percent?" I am sure that you would answer that one hundred percent is more. However, Kingdom mathematics sometimes supplies a different answer. Which would you rather have, ninety percent of your money with God's blessing (after the tithe), or one hundred percent of your finances under a curse (see Malachi 3:8-11 above). You see, ninety percent with God's blessing really does turn out to be more than one hundred percent without His blessing.

In the Bible, the tithe represents a "first fruits offering." A "first fruits offering" represented the first fruit from the harvest which was offered up to God out of thankfulness for the harvest, and in recognition of the fact that the whole harvest belonged to God. The first part, or the first fruits, represented the whole. Likewise, the tithe, or the first tenth of anything, represented the whole. When the tithe was treated as holy and given to God, then the remainder of the harvest was holy as well.

If the first piece of dough is holy, the lump (the remainder) is also.
(Romans 11:16)

When you tithe, you make all that remains in your care holy; God becomes involved in your finances since you are now partners. You may have a stack of bills sitting in front of you - but give the first tenth of your income to God and the rest of your lump becomes holy and super-naturally blessed to meet all your needs. What you have is now holy and protected by God; that is why we read in Malachi:

Bring the whole tithe into the storehouse, so that that there may be food in My house...Then I will rebuke the devourer for you...
(Malachi 3:10-11)

Because God is your partner, and your finances are holy, He will rebuke the devil from your finances as he comes to devour them in a hundred different ways. When Satan comes at you with fears and threats, you can rise up and say "I am a tither and the Bible says that therefore God will rebuke the devourer for me. God has made what I have holy and He will protect it."

God desires to bring His saving power into the financial area of your life. His promises require that you respond in faith by tithing, and when you desire, by giving of offerings cheerfully.

Giving is something that blesses us. God is not after our money; He doesn't need it. But when we give, especially sacrificially, it begins to change our hearts. God is after our hearts and our treasure is tied to our hearts. God must go through our treasure to get to our hearts. As we release our treasures we are free to give God our hearts.

Become a cheerful and gracious giver. Don't be afraid to give sacri-ficially when you feel that the Lord is directing you. God has a great blessing for you. Two weeks ago one of the women in our church felt like God was directing her to give their van to Youth Venture. At first she really struggled with it. She and her husband were involved in real estate and the market was in a terrible downturn. They had had very little income over the past six months. They needed the money from the sale of this van. But she could not shake the sense that she was to do this. She and her husband prayed over it and decided that they had to do what they felt the Lord was calling them to do. It took real faith to give away that van, but as they did it they felt the nearness and pleasure of God. The following Sunday I saw them at church. They were very excited. Unexpectedly, the husband had been offered and had accepted a new job in real estate that meant a $5,000 raise per month. As they had obeyed God, He had sent a blessing to overtake them.

This important Kingdom Key of Giving functions in every area of life, and is not limited to the giving and receiving of finances. Our Creator intended us to succeed and prosper in His Creation. He made us to be viceroys and lords over His Creation. Therefore, He wants us to function according to laws which He would teach us.

God wants us to have success in all areas, including our families, relationships, work, church life, personal habits and influence over society. Life is rigged in favor of those who believe in God and act in accordance to God's laws - laws that govern every dimension of life.

These laws are given to ensure that we can succeed, and no law is more basic to our success than the Law of Sowing and Reaping Returns.

10

The Kingdom Key of Agreement and Unity

The principle of unity and harmony is a foundational building block in God's Creation, basic to how our world works. It is one of the most powerful Kingdom Keys, and some of the Bible's promises associated with it almost defy belief. For instance, perhaps the greatest and most all-inclusive promise in the Bible is dependent upon unity and agreement.

> *Again I say to you, that if two of you agree on earth about anything that they may ask, it shall be done for them by My Father who is in heaven. For where two or three have gathered together in My name, I am there in their midst.*
>
> (Matthew 18:19-20)

Many Christians read this verse and scratch their heads. They know it is true because it is in the Bible, but it seems so foreign to their experience. What exactly does it mean? How literally are we to take it? How are we to apply it? Jesus makes a breathtaking promise but it has a catch, a requirement. That requirement is that they must be in agreement regarding their request.

Note the power associated with unity and agreement! Our heavenly Father gives us access to the most creative and powerful forces in His Kingdom *if* (note the big "IF") we can operate within this important Kingdom Key. But what exactly does Jesus mean by agreement?

First, we must realize who He was speaking to. He made this promise to His twelve disciples. Jesus had spent several years with these men, living with them and discipling them. He taught them how to share, serve, sacrifice and face danger together. They had left all behind to follow him (Mark 10:29-30) and had been willing to face death out of loyalty to Jesus (John 11:16). They certainly had come to understand what Jesus meant by unity and agreement. We will explore this later.

Second, note that in the promise above, Jesus stated that He would be in their midst. This means that to have agreement they must be in agreement with Jesus. Their request must be one that would be agreeable to Jesus. It must be according to God's Word.

This emphasis on unity and agreement runs throughout the entire Bible. The Bible associates unity and harmony with the greatest acts of creation and deliverance.

UNITY AND AGREEMENT IN THE GODHEAD

In the very first chapter of the Bible, unity and agreement are involved in God's creation of man.

> Then God said, "Let Us make man in Our image according to Our likeness..."

(Genesis 1:26)

Here it implies that God created man within the unity or harmony of the Godhead. Throughout the Bible, especially in the New Testament, we see the Trinity operating in perfect harmony and agreement.

Just as Creation involved agreement and harmony, so did the drama of redemption. For instance, Jesus said,

> ...Truly, truly, I say to you, the Son can do nothing of Himself, unless it is something He sees the Father doing, for whatever the Father does, these things the Son also does in like manner. For the Father loves the

Son, and shows Him all things that He Himself is doing…

(John 5:19-20)

Note the perfect unity and harmony of the Father and Son. Of the Holy Spirit, Jesus said:

But when He, the Spirit of truth, comes, He will guide you into all the truth; for He will not speak on His own initiative, but whatever He hears, He will speak; and He will disclose to you what is to come. He will glorify Me; for He will take of Mine and will disclose it to you.

(John 16:13-14)

Many other verses could be cited to further illustrate the perfect harmony and unity the Trinity operated in to bring us redemption.

UNITY AND THE EARLY CHURCH

The early Church was mighty and powerful through understanding this Kingdom Key of Unity and Agreement. They strove for the same unity that existed in the Trinity, the unity the disciples witnessed that Jesus had with His heavenly Father — the same love and unity that Jesus taught the twelve disciples to have for each other when He was with them. We see it again and again in the Book of Acts.

Before the day of Pentecost we find the disciples in unity and agreed in purpose:

These all (the disciples) *with one mind were continually devoting themselves to prayer, along with the women, and Mary the mother of Jesus, and with His brothers.*

(Acts 1:14)

On the day of Pentecost, we find them *"all together in one place"* (Acts 2:1). Following the tremendous events of Pentecost, we find that unity and agreement marked the early Christian community.

They were continually devoting themselves to the apostles' teaching and to fellowship, to the breaking of bread and to prayer. Everyone kept feeling a sense of awe; and many wonders and signs were taking place through the apostles. And all those who believed were together and had all things in common.

(Acts 2:42-44)

Throughout the Book of Acts, we find Christians united together and agreed in purpose; we also see the power and miracle supply of the Kingdom opened up to them. In contrast, much of the modern Church is divided, unreconciled, weak and powerless.

THE WONDER OF UNITY AND AGREEMENT

By now it should be coming clear that the power and dynamics of God's Kingdom are released when unity and agreement are present!

Even a quick study of our world shows that its Creator must be a being who values harmony and agreement. All around us nature displays an incredible balance, interdependency and harmony of functions. All the great laws of nature interact and correspond to bring about the bountiful and fruitful world we enjoy. Millions of different living organisms all work together in a great unity of purpose...to maintain the balance of nature and the integrity of the ecosystem.

Man has learned the hard lesson of how the whole system suffers loss when even one element of nature is damaged or destroyed. Each element, working in harmony with all the rest, is necessary if the system is to be of maximum potential.

THE SECRET MULTIPLIER

The spiritual Kingdom follows this same principle of harmony. It can only reach its maximum potential when all the ordained parts are functioning together in agreement and unity. The power of a family, a church or an organization grows exponentially when all its parts are operating in harmony and agreement. This great spiritual truth is recognized in Scripture.

> *But you will chase your enemies and they will fall before you by the sword; five of you will chase a hundred, and a hundred of you will chase ten thousand…*
>
> (Leviticus 26:7-8)

If you are good at math, you will notice that if five chases one hundred, then one hundred should chase two thousand. But, instead, it says that one hundred shall chase ten thousand - a number five times as great!

Why?

Because the principle of agreement and harmony multiplies our potential and effectiveness.

Each person's fruitfulness is enhanced when they are linked together in unity.

Again, Deuteronomy 32:30 says that one can chase a thousand and two can put to flight ten thousand.

Harmony and agreement are foundational Kingdom priorities for success and victory. Success becomes nearly impossible when any group or organization overlooks this multiplier factor. This is why Jesus could say:

> *If a kingdom is divided against itself, that kingdom cannot stand. If a house is divided against itself, that house will not be able to stand. If Satan* (i.e., Satan's kingdom) *has risen up against himself and is divided, he cannot stand, but he is finished!*
>
> (Mark 3:24-26)

DISAGREEMENT LEADS TO FAILURE

There is a negative side to the Kingdom principle of agreement: Disagreement unleashes a powerful destructive force.

Unity results in strength; a lack of unity produces weakness.

Satan attacks the churches and other godly organizations by sowing seeds of disunity, disharmony and disagreement. He does this by exploiting our natural, sinful tendencies for selfishness, pride and envy. To overcome his attacks, it is necessary for church members to humble themselves before God, and, for Christ's sake, work to restore unity.

Jesus does not allow disunity and disharmony amongst His followers.

Therefore if you are presenting your offering at the altar, and there remember that your brother has something against you, leave your offering there before the altar and go; first be reconciled to your brother, and then come and present your offering.

(Matthew 5:23-24)

Notice that unity and agreement are so important to God, and so central to His purposes for the Church, that they can take precedence even over our worship!

If someone is living in sinful disharmony with the rest of the congregation, then Jesus requires the church work carefully with that individual to restore him to unity and agreement (or else dis-fellowship him or her). One of the purposes of church discipline, or excommunication, is to allow the remaining members to function in agreement and unity. Only in this way can the church maintain her authority and power.

If your brother sins, go and show him his fault in private; if he listens to you, you have won your brother. But if he does not listen to you, take one or two more with you, so that BY THE MOUTH OF TWO OR THREE WITNESSES EVERY FACT MAY BE CONFIRMED.

If he refuses to listen to them, tell it to the church; and if he refuses to listen even to the church, let him be to you as a Gentile and a tax collector.

(Matthew 18:15-17)

Preserving unity is not only an important priority, it is difficult. It is hard work to confront people in wisdom and patience. It is far easier to turn a cold shoulder and become indifferent to those you disagree with than to sit down with them and work it out. Only when people understand how important unity is will they humble themselves and do what it takes to maintain it.

Disharmony within the Body, or disloyalty to Jesus, cannot be ignored. As agreement and unity are lost in a church, that church begins to lose the supernatural dimension, becoming just another social club. It is always a great mistake to settle for a superficial tranquility over the power of true agreement and unity.

The wonderful promise we used to open this chapter appears just two verses later in Matthew 18:19. This shows us that the agreement Jesus was talking about is not simply a superficial prayer of agreement, but instead involves an entire lifestyle of true agreement.

Let's look again at that promise.

Again I say to you, that if two of you agree on earth about anything that they may ask, it shall be done for them by My Father who is in heaven. For where two or three have gathered together in My name, I am there in their midst.

(Matthew 18:19-20)

Look carefully at the word *agree* in verse 19. It is the Greek word *sumphoneo* which means "to sound together, to be in accord or to bargain" (that is, to negotiate to the point of agreement).

LESSONS FROM THE SYMPHONY

Some of you may have noticed that we get our English word symphony from this Greek word *sumphoneo*. A symphony is an arrangement of musical instruments that makes beautiful music when all the instruments are in the same key, playing the same song, blending and working together. Symphony music requires long hours of practice together to reach true harmony. Even one instrument out of harmony can ruin the effect.

In the same way, spiritual agreement depends upon real and meaningful unity existing between those doing the praying. It is more than simply getting a group of independent and apathetic Christians together to pray a prayer, and then add on at the end of the prayer, "And we agree together in Jesus' name in accordance with Matthew 18:19."

Prayer demands the kind of agreement practiced by the early Christians in the Book of Acts; every Christian made the advancement of God's Kingdom the first priority of their life; they worked together for the good of all, even freely sharing their possessions with Christians in need!

That is the kind of agreement it takes to make the promise of Matthew 18:19 truly effective!

FOOTHILLS PROSPERED THROUGH UNITY AND AGREEMENT

The history of Foothills Christian Church is a testimony to the power of this principle. Foothills began as two very small, separate groups, each about a dozen people when they first started. One group, led by my brother, David, was affiliated as a church plant with the Christian and Missionary Alliance. The second group, led by me, started later, and was a church plant loosely affiliated with the Vineyard movement.

Each group experienced moderate growth.

Each group was very different from the other.

Each had unique gifts.

One group had good organization and programs, a clear identity, and a strong leadership. The other group had anointed worship, a freedom to minister in the Holy Spirit, and a tradition of emphasis on home groups. While each had clear areas of strengths, each also had real areas of weakness. In fact, one group's strengths tended to correlate to the other group's weaknesses.

Dave and I gradually came to see the limitations of our individual fellowships. It became clear that each of them was lacking in certain elements they needed to succeed. At the same time, we could see that one fellowship had the ingredients the other was missing. God showed us that if we would agree to die to our independence and autonomy, and come into agreement and unite together, His highest purposes for our fellowships could be accomplished.

Bringing together two groups, on the surface so very different, was not easy. Nor was the integration of two pastors, quite different in temperament and gifting, automatic. But because we believed in the power of agreement and unity, we worked, bargained and compromised together until we had the new fellowship in place.

From the beginning, we understood that each fellowship had to die for true agreement in the new one to grow. This required real grace and humility on the part of all involved. People who once had visibility and leadership had to move aside and make room for others from the other fellowship. Everyone renegotiated their place and position.

We had been warned by many church leaders and pastors not to undertake such a move.

"Mergers usually blow up," they said.

In fact, Dave and I had never really seen one that was successful. But we knew that what we were attempting wasn't a merger - it was the death of two fellowships to create a new one. We trusted God to resurrect those elements from each fellowship that He wanted in the new church. We truly had to lay it all down to see what God would bring about through our unity and agreement.

As a result, there was very little disruption or disagreement among the members of either of the fellowships. More importantly, **we have accomplished far more together than our sum total would have been had we stayed separate.** In the past twenty years, the church has grown by 2000 percent, and many ministries, including several schools, community centers, campus Bible clubs, and two drug and alcohol treatment centers as well as many other community-impacting efforts, have gotten underway. By joining together, we not only received each other's gifts, we also tapped into the power of unity and agreement.

We multiplied our effectiveness by coming together.

THE POWER OF SYNERGY

In the natural world we have a name for this multiplying phenomenon: We call it synergy.

SYNERGY IS THE MULTIPLIER EFFECT OF THINGS WORKING TOGETHER.

For instance, two generators working on line with each other will produce more power than the total power of both working independently. In fact, two generators working in line produce the same as four working independently, and four working in line do the work of sixteen. Even more incredible is the well-established fact that one draft horse working alone can pull two tons, but two working together can pull an incredible twenty-three tons!

Synergy is effective in <u>all</u> realms!

For instance, music groups like the Beatles and Rolling Stones and U-

2 added up to much more together than if you just considered the solo abilities of the individuals involved. In each case, none of their solo efforts ever even came close to what they produced together.

Sometimes, synergy is summed up by these words: "The whole is greater than the sum of its parts."

Synergy also works in the realm of the Kingdom of God. The Billy Graham evangelistic team illustrates this. Some forty-five years ago this group of men heard a call from God early in their adulthood, and they banded together with Billy Graham to pursue the goal of world evangelization. Most of that early team remained together for fifty years. The results of their unity and agreement have been miraculous.

IT WORKS FOR FAMILIES

I can personally testify to the blessing and strength that come when a marriage is in unity and agreement. My marriage and home life have been a constant source of strength, blessing and agreement, not only to my wife and me, but to our three sons as well. On the other hand, many can give testimony to the suffering and loss that takes place when marriage partners are not in harmony and unity.

Agreement and unity in families produces a multiplier effect. The achievements of such families as the Kennedys, Rockefellers and Bushes illustrate how powerful this effect can be. Of course, thousands of families less famous also demonstrate this principle by the achievements of their children. By teaching all family members, starting with Mom and Dad, to die to self in the interest of some great goal (like the Kingdom of God), will allow a unity and harmony to develop that will unleash the incredible multiplier effect of synergy in the lives of the children. Family members will encourage and cheer each other on in every effort and victory, rather than become jealous and threatened. Rather than try to undercut and undermine each other, family members will each build off the momentum of the victories of the others for the common good.

Every achievement and victory by any individual will strengthen and multiply every other member of your family.

Jonathan Edwards was one of the greatest Church leaders in American history; he was the product of a home with harmony and godliness (his father was a minister). More than 400 descendants of this godly home have been traced. They include one hundred professors (including fourteen college presidents); one hundred ministers, missionaries or theologians; one hundred lawyers and judges; and sixty doctors, authors or editors.

Unfortunately, examples of pathological family trees of failure can be demonstrated to flow from homes of self-centeredness and disunity as well.

This very powerful principle of unity and harmony is a secret to God's Creation (both visible and invisible). Understanding it, and working in conjunction with this law will produce dramatic results, just like understanding and harnessing the power of electricity revolutionized modern life. We cannot ignore this powerful Kingdom Key and expect to gain victory in our lives.

APPLY THIS PRINCIPLE ON THREE LEVELS

Agreement and unity must operate on three levels.

First, it must operate on the personal level.

You must be unified within yourself. The Bible says a double-minded man is "unstable in all his ways" (James 1:8). "Double-minded" means a person is internally divided in their goals, plans, values or loyalties. Such a person is guaranteed frustration, and, in the end, failure, because he is a "house divided" (this is the unenviable position of a backslidden Christian).

Jesus taught that we must consider well our decisions, to "count the cost" before making our goals. He spoke of men building towers, and kings going out to war who must first determine whether they have the resolve and resources to finish the job, lest they fail in the attempt (Luke 14:28-32).

We must have an inner unity of purpose before we attempt difficult goals. The Bible calls this being "single minded."

Second, we must operate in agreement on the interpersonal level.

We must be in agreement with the members of the social unit we are involved in. This could be a marriage, family, church or any other organization or grouping. Any organization lacking unity is crippled and rendered powerless, no matter how large. In fact, groups can actually become more powerful and influential even as they become smaller through defections and purges, as long as those who remain are in true agreement.

Unity and agreement are so essential to success that all must equally be determined to reach this goal of unity. It is in the best interests of all members to humble themselves, forgive, negotiate and sacrifice to reach unity and agreement. Only then will the MULTIPLIER EFFECT manifest itself.

A third level of agreement must be reached to ensure that a godly, rather than a diabolical, end is achieved: We must be in agreement with God and His Word!

The power of God's Kingdom is only released when we come into agreement with God and operate in harmony with His will and laws. However it is possible to achieve huge objectives by agreement on merely the first two levels. Remember, God introduced the many languages at the tower of Babel to frustrate agreement on two levels only. The peoples of the earth had united, in defiance of God, to build a great city and tower to glorify their greatness (and probably for pagan religious worship). God acted in mercy before their rebellion could become too great.

The LORD came down to see the city and the tower which the sons of men had built. The LORD said, "Behold, they are one people, and they all have the same language. And this is what they began to do, and now nothing which they purpose to do will be impossible for them. Come, let Us go down and there confuse their language, so that they will not understand one another's speech."

(Genesis 11:5-7)

God was merciful to act because when people act in unity and agreement outside of God's will and Word, great tragedy and suffering can result.

The rise of the Nazi party to power and near world domination resulted from great harmony on the first two levels. The same was true when Communism successfully replaced numerous world governments. A more current example is the increasing power of the gay lobby in our own country. Through being focused and agreed on their agenda, the homosexual community, although a small group, has achieved tremendous power and brought about destructive change.

As Christians, we must be sure that all of our unity and agreement with others is built upon agreement with God and His Word. This puts a limit on just what we can negotiate in order to come into agreement with others.

We simply must have some biblical non-negotiables.

If we link the incredible Kingdom Key of Agreement and Unity with the others we have studied, such as the Key of Active Faith and the Key of Diligence, and put them into practice, we will have <u>unlimited</u> power and potential. In this way we can begin to see answers to the prayer Jesus taught us to pray, that *"Your kingdom come Your will be done, On earth as it is in heaven"* (Matthew 6:10).

11

The Kingdom Key of Vision

Where there is no vision, the people perish.

(Proverbs 29:18, KJV)

VISION IS ESSENTIAL!

The above verse points out the importance of vision for human life. It is not merely an option, it is essential, if humans are to increase, succeed and prosper against the ever-present realities of destruction and decay. A lack of vision leads to apathy, deception and deterioration among individuals, families and whole societies.

But what exactly is vision? Why is it essential to life? Why will you ultimately fail without it?

Vision may be defined as a God-inspired view of not only the world and the circumstances around you, but also of God's purposes in those circumstances. Further, it includes understanding your role in the accomplishment of those same purposes. Vision allows you to see circumstances from God's perspective and understand how you fit in.

The Hebrew word translated as *vision* in the above verse is *chazown*, which comes from the root word *chaza*, meaning "to split or divide." It also has a secondary meaning of "to see or behold." Vision is the sight one receives as one splits or divides the surface circumstances and peers beyond them into the hidden, deeper (or spiritual) realities.

Vision gives meaning and fulfillment to life. When you have vision you will feel and live far differently. You realize that you are God's partner in bringing about a better future.

Whenever I drive by people on my way to church who are mowing their lawns, washing their cars or preparing for a day at the beach, I always feel sad for them that they have no real vision. Sunday is not a special day to them. They have nothing more important to do than to hang out at the park or take their dog to a dog show. They are not living life in partnership with God. They haven't received His vision.

God wants us to have vision for our lives, to have some understanding of our purpose and calling. Vision gives every area of our lives dignity and meaning.

We should have vision for our marriages, something that makes them of great consequence and importance. God wants to give us vision for our children, that is, some God-ordained picture of their special gifts and their God-ordained trajectory and destiny. God wants us to have vision for our careers, workplaces or schools. Vision will lift these out of the mundane.

The story is told of the time that Sir Christopher Wren was building one of the great cathedrals in England. It was an endeavor that took many years. At one point when work was going especially slow, he decided to visit the worksite and look in among the workers. He disguised his dress so he could go among them unrecognized. Most of the workers looked unmotivated and worked with little enthusiasm. He approached different workers and conversed with them. He would ask them what they were doing. One replied, "I'm cutting stones to fit into a wall." Another said "I'm building a scaffolding." Finally he spotted one man who was whistling happily and working with gusto. He approached him and also asked him "What is it you are doing?" He replied "I'm helping Sir Christopher Wren build the greatest cathedral in all of England." Vision makes all the difference in how we live.

Our vocation should be more than just a paycheck. Our time at school should be more than just a paper chase for a diploma. Wherever we are and whatever we are doing, God has a purpose in it. Ask yourself, why does a sovereign God have you where He has you? Why does He have you doing what you are doing? What is His purpose? Vision changes everything.

God wants to develop within us a vision for our local church, our community and nation.

In all these areas, we must see beyond the mundane and shallow and grasp God's purposes and possibilities.

Without this vision, our lives mean little. Our enthusiasm, attitudes and courage shrivel. Our lives lose nobility. We tend to become small, petty and selfish. People are overcome by vices, marriages unravel, families disintegrate and societies decline.

Where there is no vision, the people perish.

(Proverbs 29:18, KJV)

Perish comes from the Hebrew word *para* which means "to let loose or let go." Without vision, people begin to let themselves go, to decline and slide downward.

This principle is true for individuals and nations.

THE EXAMPLE OF AMERICA

America, at one time, saw herself as a nation of destiny. We believed we were "one nation under God," conceived to be a light to the nations. We were the birthplace of a grand new experiment called "democracy," where men and women, who, because they were each submitted to a divine King, could be entrusted with unprecedented liberties, free from the rule of human kings and tyrants. We believed we were placed in a "new world" to establish a nation upon Christian principles which would launch the gospel around the world!

With such a grand vision, America quickly became, by almost any measurement, the greatest nation that ever existed. Unfortunately, many of our leaders and thinkers became intoxicated with our success and wealth, and they forgot the God of our youth, betraying democracy to instead rule as an oligarchy (rule by the elite few). By seizing control of the educational centers, and through intimidation and politics, they virtually eliminated dissenting thought (a process that continues today).

Next, they gained control of the Supreme Court and began to rule this nation by judicial decree. Beginning in the late '50s and early '60s, they began a process of recreating America in their own image: a secular America, an America without a transcendent vision given it by a transcendent Being.

Today we are eating the bitter fruit of this change.

From the late '60s, America has increasingly lost her sense of vision and destiny. Our nation has fragmented, and individuals have increasingly begun to live only for the moment and only for themselves.

America has gone into a steep decline. Our marriages and families break apart, our schools and institutions decay, and our citizens increasingly become enslaved to addictions, compulsions and self-destruction.

We have begun "to perish."

WE WERE MADE FOR VISION

People, as well as entire societies, do not live well without vision. To try to do so is a violation of our God-given human nature, and a denial of our human spirit.

Helen Keller, herself blind and deaf, was once asked if there was anything worse than being blind. "Yes," she answered, "to be able to see but to have no vision."

Only true vision gives meaning and enduring direction to our lives. Apart from vision, we cannot enjoy lasting and true fulfillment. On the day God made mankind, He gave us an all-encompassing vision of breathtaking proportions:

> *...fill the earth, and subdue it; and rule over...every living thing that moves on the earth.*
>
> (Genesis 1:28)

This mandate or vision to rule the earth for the glory of God has never been suspended. In fact, it has been expanded!

Jesus told His small band of followers:

> *All authority has been given to Me in heaven and on earth. Go therefore and make disciples of all the nations...teaching them to observe all that I commanded you...*
>
> (Matthew 28:18-20)

It is within this background of breathtaking destiny that our own lives begin to assume a unique dignity and purpose. Vision and destiny are not just given to us as the human race, or as a Christian people...they are also uniquely given to each individual.

Each person must discover the unique purpose, gifts and opportunities to which they are called. An individual will never attain true fulfillment, happiness or full potential until they have a God-given vision.

When I was a young man, I drifted from job to job. I was also a student at college and drifted from class to class, changing my major several times.

I could not get excited about anything in life.

Mostly, I just hung out at the beach.

Unlike my parents' generation, which had undergone the Great Depression, I was not driven to acquire money, property or financial security. Nothing seemed to grab my imagination. Because of the empty and insipid worldview I acquired while attending our spiritually and morally bankrupt public schools and colleges, any sense of destiny or vision I might have had was lost.

I emotionally dropped out. I was apathetic about everything except escaping the emptiness inside through quick thrills, entertainment, drugs and alcohol. I went on a long moral downslide; I stopped caring, becoming a classic underachiever.

When I was twenty-three, I had a powerful encounter with the Lord Jesus Christ and was born again. In an instant, the depression and apathy were broken. I suddenly realized that the philosophies I had been taught in school were a contemptible lie.

Life did have a purpose and a point! Life was a venture that indeed deserved our best efforts; in fact, it cried out for heroic efforts.

Immediately, my attitude changed. I quit drinking and using drugs, my grade point average rose two whole points, my interest in people, history and politics (in fact, my interest in everything) was ignited! Although I did not yet have a specific vision for my life, the broad outlines were falling into place.

I discovered that I was uniquely created by a Supreme Being who knew even the number of hairs on my head. He knew me by name before I was born, and had uniquely created and gifted me for a special purpose. The specifics of the vision would gradually be added as I continued to walk with Him.

Many people wonder if God does in fact have a personal vision for them, a personal call for them to fulfill. I believe the Bible teaches that we do. In Ephesians we read:

For we are His workmanship, created in Christ Jesus for good works,
which God prepared beforehand so that we would walk in them.
(Ephesians 2:10)

This verse tells us, first of all, that we are God's *"workmanship."* The Greek word is the word *poiema* which literally can mean "work of art" (some translations interpret the word this way). We get the English word "poem" from this word. Like a poem or a work of art, each of our lives is individually crafted to be a message of God's love and greatness to the world.

This message is delivered as we discover our purpose. It says that we all were *"...created in Christ Jesus for good works, which God prepared beforehand..."* These *"good works"* which were prepared beforehand for us to *"walk in"* I like to call "divine achievements" that we have been called to accomplish in partnership with God.

Every one of us has been specially created and gifted to accomplish these "divine achievements." This is the vision for our lives that only God can give us. As we walk with God and submit to the ministry of the church and its leadership, we begin to receive this vision for our lives. God has a vision for every life that is marvelous, even for those that the world might label "disadvantaged" or "severely handicapped."

Every life is a work of art.

Every life has a divine purpose.

Many lives today are like mine was. They suffer from a lack of vision. They drift through an empty, unfulfilling existence because they have no vision. They are constantly disappointed because they do not know what they want or where they want to go, so they end up in places or circumstances they would have never chosen.

Life just happens to them.

Only vision gives you direction and allows you to choose your destination. Otherwise, life is determined by accidents, happenstance and outside pressures.

A lack of vision is an epidemic problem in our day. Our youth lack purpose or direction, so they aimlessly drift through life, distracting themselves with self destructive behaviors. Amusement and physical stimulation substitute for dreams and accomplishment.

Even many churches lack vision. Rather than boldly seek God for inspiration and vision, they fill their hearts with vision-stealing negative thoughts. Pastors talk among themselves: "This is the hardest town to minister in," or "This town is a preacher's graveyard," or "This is such an ungodly generation, a very hard generation in which to minister."

The people in the pews say, "People today just do not want to hear the gospel; they have everything they think they need," or "I am just not gifted for evangelism. I will just get tongue tied if I try to share," or "Well, what can we do, things just will get worse and worse anyway."

On and on it goes, until we have nullified all of God's great promises to us concerning the power of His Word and of His Kingdom, disqualifying ourselves from receiving vision.

GOD-GIVEN VISION BRINGS DELIVERANCE

God's Word tells us that it is the God-given vision that comes when people accept God's Word which will deliver them, and whole societies, from apathy, aimlessness and destruction.

He sent His word and healed them, And delivered them from their destructions.

(Psalm 107:20)

Oh, that America would once again embrace God's Word, that we might be healed as a nation! But first our churches, pulpits and Christian families must embrace God's Word over every area of life. Only then will see clearly and receive God-given vision.

God has promised to restore a broken and afflicted people by giving vision. He spoke to Israel during times of national decline and promised future restoration by granting its people vision:

> *It will come about after this That I will pour out My Spirit on all mankind: And your sons and daughters will prophesy, Your old men will dream dreams, Your young men will see visions.*
>
> (Joel 2:28; Acts 2:17)

The people who will change the world are the people who have vision. The future belongs to people who have vision because they will define the future. The apostle Paul was a man who changed the world because he was a man driven to fulfill a vision for ministry that God had entrusted to him.

> *...I press on so that I may lay hold of that for which also I was laid hold of by Christ Jesus...forgetting what lies behind and reaching forward to what lies ahead, I press on toward the goal of the upward call of God in Christ Jesus.*
>
> (Philippians 3:12-14)

Paul had God-given vision - a goal to pursue. It was this vision that energized Paul's life, giving it meaning and stature. It was this vision that freed him from the wounds, guilt and foolishness of the past. It directed and inspired him. It was this vision that gave him joy and fulfillment. Paul never allowed himself to be distracted from it so that at the end of his life he could testify to King Agrippa:

> *So, King Agrippa, I did not prove disobedient to the heavenly vision.*
>
> (Acts 26:19)

What our families, our churches, our society and our nation are dying for is not more welfare programs, better education or even universal health care. The great need of the hour, the only hope, is men and women with God-given vision!

Vision allows people to see things not merely as they are...but as God would make them.

God-given vision lifts us above the negative.

It ignites us out of apathy.

It propels us past the limitations of man and into the very possibilities of God!

It is more than simply believing that God can. Vision is an inner conviction so clear that we can almost see it. Vision allows us to see the invisible and work to make it a concrete reality.

For we walk by faith, not by sight.

(2 Corinthians 5:7)

How to Reach Your God-given Potential

If you want to be more than you are in life, if you want to be a better person, you must first find the answer the following question: "Just what is it that makes some people rise above the crowd to become the very best that people can be?"

In my opinion, the answer is *vision.*

Great human beings are not born, they are created by the visions they hold. We can never rise above the level of our vision (or lack of it).

George Barna, researcher and church historian, has pointed out that the tiny Albanian woman who today we know as "Mother Teresa" was not in any way special in her early life. In her early years in the convent, she did not stand out as a student, a leader of her peers, or even as an especially pious woman. However, after years of prayer and waiting on God, a vision was born within her that stretched her and inspired her to great acts. Today she is known and admired throughout the world by kings and presidents, not because she was born a great woman, but because she was given a great vision.[3]

Great visions do not come from great people; great visions make people great.

Visions inspire, energize and direct ordinary people to become extraordinary.

In the end, your life will be measured by how much of God's vision you were able to grasp. The legacy you leave your children will be no greater than the vision you hold in your spirit. Your influence for good as a parent, Christian, coworker, businessman, or citizen will rise no higher than your vision.

Consider the great heroes of the Bible, people who made tremendous contributions to the world of their time. In fact, through their writings or examples they continue to exert an influence for good even in our modern day. These people gained divine approval and now enjoy their eternal reward with God.

What was their secret? What made them men and women who are still loved and revered to the very present? After all, most of them were merely shepherds, farmers and fishermen.

The answer is everywhere written in Scripture: It was the Word of God, and a vision from God that elevated their lives. The autobiographical statement by Amos shows he was just an everyday person who was elevated by God's vision.

The words of Amos, who was among the sheepherders from Tekoa, which he envisioned in visions concerning Israel in the days of Uzziah king of Judah...

(Amos 1:1)

I am not a prophet, nor am I the son of a prophet; for I am a herdsman and a grower of sycamore figs. But the LORD took me from following the flock and the LORD said to me, "Go prophesy to My people Israel."

(Amos 7:14-15)

Throughout the Bible, ordinary people were made extraordinary through a vision from God.

In the days before Samuel, we find Israel in a period of steep decline because of a lack of vision; the people were perishing.

Now the boy Samuel was ministering to the LORD before Eli. And word from the Lord was rare in those days, visions were infrequent.

(1 Samuel 3:1)

God would begin to bring deliverance to His oppressed and defeated people by giving Samuel God-given vision. It was a lack of vision, brought about by their sinfulness and disobedience, which was responsible for their predicament. By the granting of vision, we see in this very same chapter of 1 Samuel that deliverance begins.

CAN ANYONE RECEIVE VISION?

Throughout the Old Testament we read the phrase "and the word of the Lord came to" dozens and dozens of times. This marked the call of God to make a person His prophetic voice to the people. Likewise, in the New Testament, people are called personally to follow Jesus, and they receive a personal calling to serve God's purposes. The great difference between the Old Testament and the New Testament is that vision was only given to certain special individuals in the Old Testament, like prophets and kings, while in the New Testament God's Spirit is poured out upon all flesh. (Acts 2:17)

The New Testament boldly declares:

For all who are being led by the Spirit of God, these are sons of God.
(Romans 8:14)

All Bible scholars agree that this was the primary importance of Pentecost: All of God's people could now receive the vision and anointing that, in the Old Testament, were reserved for prophets, priests and kings.

Think of what this means for you!

It means God wants to elevate and make noble your life by the development of God-given vision.

Through you, He wants to bless and heal those around you. Remember, it is not lack of education, family upbringing or the present circumstances that limit your life; rather, it is your vision (or a lack of it). God-given vision, more than anything else, defines and determines the impact and importance of a person, a family, church, business or country.

GAINING VISION

Vision may come suddenly in a dramatic way through a dream or vision, but more often it will come as a growing conviction. It may be nothing more than a growing sense of God-given faith that you can accomplish something.

Vision involves the future; however, it is built upon the present and the past. Therefore, we can assist in developing our vision by asking certain questions.

What special burdens has God placed on my heart?

How is God using me now?

In what ministries or activities do I especially sense the blessing and presence of God's enabling Spirit in my life?

What clue concerning my call and vision might I find in the natural and spiritual gifts that God has given me?

What prophecies may have been spoken over my life? What strengths and potentials have spiritual or vocational leaders pointed out and encouraged in me?

In considering the family I was born into, the education I received and the experiences and training that a sovereign God allowed in my life, what clues might they give in shedding light on what my purpose might be?

In carefully and prayerfully considering these questions, we can begin to gain understanding and help clarify our purpose and the call of God on our lives. The input of mentors and spiritual leaders at this point is critical.

Remember, true vision develops over time.

It can't be rushed. Like a chicken and its egg, we must be willing to incubate the vision and be patient. We can't be demanding of God or others once we think we have a vision. We need to wait on God and the vision until it develops more and more clearly and we are prepared for it.

In some cases, this may take many years. At the right time, God Himself will open the right doors.

We have not even begun to clarify the vision until we can write it down clearly and plainly. Writing it down helps us understand it and to be patient and steadfast through any delays or testings.

...Record the vision And inscribe it on tablets, That the one who reads it may run. For the vision is yet for the appointed time; It hastens toward the goal and it will not fail Though it tarries, wait for it; For it will certainly come, it will not delay.

(Habakkuk 2:2-3)

EMBRACING THE VISION

Vision is always bigger than you.

It must stretch you as a person.

It changes you and enlarges you.

While it is exciting, even thrilling, to begin to receive a vision, it is also a sobering thing. To see that vision fulfilled, God will have to prepare you and transform you. There will be struggle, hardship and disappointment. The vision will mark your life. Someone said once that "It's not so that we have a vision, it's more like a vision has us."

True vision cannot be easily escaped just because things are difficult or hard. Even in those times, God-given vision continues to haunt us. It does not surrender or leave us alone, but continues to drive us to our very best, even beyond our very best, until the fulfillment is attained.

In the Bible, Joseph is a clear picture of this. Although he was the youngest in his family, God gave him a vision that would eventually culminate in saving not only his entire family and kinsmen, but all of Egypt.

God had a plan to raise up a nation within the nation of Egypt. He would make a nation of several million people from the twelve sons of Israel using Egypt as the womb or incubator. But to do it, He would have to develop a great leader to go before them. He made Joseph into that kind of a leader by the vision that He put deep within him, and then orchestrating his life to develop the character necessary to fulfill the job.

It was the God-given vision that stayed Joseph's course and caused him to triumph over betrayal, enslavement and prison. The vision and dealings of God were forming the man. Psalm 105 outlines how God purposed to develop Joseph as His instrument.

> *And He called for a famine upon the land; He broke the whole staff of bread. He sent a man before them, Joseph, who was sold as a slave. They afflicted his feet with fetters; He himself was laid in irons. Until the time that his word came to pass, the word of the LORD tested him.*
>
> (Psalm 105:16-19)

Can you imagine the agonies of Joseph?

The word or vision he received from God must have seemed like an impossible dream, a cruel joke. He must have been tempted to doubt it and throw it away.

It tested him and stretched him; it continued to return to him, and empowered him to rise after every blow and overcome every setback. In effect, it made him. In the same way, we must realize that every word we receive from God will be tested. It is one of the ways God uses to develop faith and humility in us, to prepare us to be good stewards of the fulfillment when it comes.

All vision must be tested and proven. It is this testing which separates God-given vision from mere fleshly ambition and presumption. It is this testing which purifies the dream and vision from that which is not of God, and prepares us to receive the fulfillment of the dream.

Our vision will lead us through the valley of testing. It is in this valley that we will either quit or surrender the vision in the face of difficulty and doubt, or we will pass the test and inherit the blessing.

For you have need of endurance, so that when you have done the will of God, you may receive what was promised.

(Hebrews 10:36)

God wants to plant vision in your life and have you hold on to it, despite testings and circumstances, until you can rejoice in the fulfillment.

A VISION FOR CHILDREN

My mother is for me an inspiring example of vision. From the time her five children were young, she had a vision that they would serve God. Every night she would read us Bible stories. She would frequently tell us that God had plans for us, and that His hand was on our lives. Everyday, while she worked around the house, she would pray for her children. If I have one picture of my mother that stands out above all the others, it is of her praying for her children.

The entrance of her eldest children into the teen years coincided with the social and spiritual upheaval of the '60s and '70s. We were caught up in drugs, revolution and the promiscuity of the public school campuses. New philosophies filled our heads. By the time of our twentieth birthdays, each of us was addicted to drugs and alcohol.

None of us had any vision for life.

I am sure my mother was tempted to quit praying. She must have been discouraged. All of her efforts in raising us and praying for us must have looked wasted. Yet, the vision inspired her to continue to pray for her children.

Gradually, God tracked down the prodigals, and in the midst of our own self-made destructions, God dramatically broke through to reach us. Now, my mother is enjoying the fulfillment of her vision. Three of her five children are in full-time ministry. When I consider the events of my life, I credit my mother and her prayers more than any other thing for the blessings I now enjoy.

YOUR PERSONAL VISION

What vision is God wanting to develop in your heart and soul? What great thing does He want to bring about through you? Are you perhaps being led through the valley of testings? Are you tempted to fall short of God's call on your life? Are you honoring God's call to you?

Perhaps God wants to speak to you about your children, to give you vision for them. Perhaps He wants to speak to you about having vision for your church or your community or something in the area of your vocational field. Follow the example of my mother, who followed the example of another mother in the New Testament, when God began to give her vision for her son.

But Mary treasured all these things, pondering them in her heart...and His mother treasured all these things in her heart.

(Luke 2:19, 51)

When God spoke to Mary concerning her son, Jesus, she made that vision the treasure of her heart. She pondered the meaning of it. Like a woman taking out her treasured jewelry and gazing at it and enjoying it, Mary would frequently take out the vision and promises of God from her heart where she had stored them and turn them over in her mind, filling her imagination with what they might mean. Everyday the vision grew in her, strengthening her as she went about her tasks, bringing joy into her life.

Let your vision from God, as it develops, become the treasure of your heart, one that is never far from your thoughts or dreams.

It will enlarge your life.

Begin to pray to God, asking Him for vision for your life. Do not be afraid to become a great person for God. Begin to make the things God has already shown you the treasure of your life.

Thank God for what He has already given you.

Think and meditate upon these things. God works through vision. It is one of the great Keys by which His Kingdom power and riches are released. In the next chapter, we will explore the role of imagination in the development of vision.

12

The Kingdom Key of Inspired Imagination

UNDERSTANDING THE ROLE OF IMAGINATION IN GOD-GIVEN VISION

Let the words of my mouth and the meditation of my heart Be acceptable in Your sight, O LORD, my rock and my Redeemer.

(Psalm 19:14)

In the last chapter we studied the importance of having vision. This chapter focuses on how we can prepare ourselves to receive God-given vision. To understand the process, we must first know how God uses our imagination.

Vision is dependent upon imagination. In the above scripture, the psalmist, understanding the vital importance of the meditations (or imaginings) of the heart, asks God to help him at the level of his imagination.

Vision must be something that we can see and conceive of in our imagination. Whatever fills our imagination will eventually become our vision for life - be it good or evil. We can state the Kingdom Key of Imagination this way:

Whatever controls our imagination will determine our vision, producing the eventual fruit of our lives.

Read the above sentence over again slowly until you fully grasp the power of this Kingdom principle. The greatest determining factor of our lives is not our environment, our upbringing, our sex or race, or the economy. Rather, it is the imaginations of our hearts. Concerning this Jesus said:

...Listen to Me, all of you, and understand: there is nothing outside the man which can defile him if it goes into him; but the things which proceed out of the man are what defile the man.

(Mark 7:14-15)

Jesus taught, in contrast to modern humanists, that it is not what goes into a man (i.e., his environment) that defiles or corrupts him, but what comes out of him, that is, out of the imaginations of his heart. People are not defeated or disqualified from blessing because of where they were born or what others have done to them, but rather by what they allow to become the imaginations of their heart.

Have you not known two people who have come from exactly the same environment, even the same family, yet whose lives ended up radically different? The difference began at the level of the imaginations of their heart.

All our words and actions reflect the imaginations of our heart. Our words, even the ones we speak carelessly, reveal the images of our heart. For this reason Jesus said our hearts can be judged by the words we speak in unguarded moments.

For out of the abundance of the heart the mouth speaks... I say to you that for every idle word men may speak, they will give account of it in the day of judgment.

(Matthew 12:34, 36, NKJ)

IMAGINATIONS LEAD TO ACTIONS

Jesus taught us that if we want to see lasting change in our lives, we must begin with our imaginations.

Take care what you listen to (that is what you receive into your heart). *By your standard of measure it will be measured to you; and more shall be given you besides.*

(Mark 4:24)

When you listen to and accept something as being true, it goes into your heart and begins to form a lens by which you will view and evaluate everything else. It becomes a standard by which you judge others' actions and by which you determine what is likely or possible. When we accept untruths and distortions then our lens and standards become distorted and our evaluations and expectations become twisted. We become a negative self-fulfilling prophecy.

Jesus knew we would tend to make life conform to what we imagined in our hearts. Also, our level of faith and vision would be limited by the imaginations of our hearts. Therefore, He urged the utmost care in the realm of our imagination.

Instead of simply allowing anything to come into our imagination, we should cultivate a godly and fruitful imagination. The Bible has long counseled this:

Watch over your heart with all diligence, For from it flow the springs of life.

(Proverbs 4:23)

The heart is where failure, breakdown and dishonor begin for many people. Their imagination is a junkyard of worthless and vain imaginings that will come to shape their lives. They did not watch over their heart with all diligence and failed to take care what they listened to. Of the wicked, the Bible says:

The imaginations of their heart run riot.

(Psalm 73:7)

For many people, their imaginations lack restraint and are filled with evil. These evil imaginings eventually give rise to evil deeds. When a person's imagination is full of wrong pictures and visions, they are sure to be overcome by them.

There is never outward failure until there has first been inward failure. Likewise, outward success will also follow inward success. Truth in the imaginings of the heart, coupled with godly character, will always produce success in God's world. The reverse is also true.

Remember, God destroyed the world when mankind's imaginations became completely filled with evil. At that point, mankind was capable only of doing more evil.

And God saw that the wickedness of man was great in the earth, and that every imagination of the thoughts of his heart was only evil continually. And it repented the LORD that he had made man on the earth, and it grieved him at his heart. And the LORD said, I will destroy man…from the face of the earth.

(Genesis 6:5-7, KJV)

Likewise, our culture has grown corrupted because people have polluted their imaginations. People have saturated their imaginations with countless hours of viewing pornographic websites, violent movies, celebrity gossip television shows and glamour magazines. As a result, we have increasingly fallen into shallowness, sensuality, adultery, divorce, violence and perversion. Remember, we eventually act out what we fill our imaginations with.

VAIN IMAGINATIONS

But Christians must do more than simply avoid putting evil before their eyes. We must present our imaginations to God. Many Christians simply do not realize the importance of imagination, and do not understand the importance of cultivating an imagination that would give birth to God-given vision.

The Bible talks about the difference between our own fleshly imaginations (what the Bible sometimes calls "vain imaginations" or "foolish imaginations") and true vision that God develops in our imagination.

Vain or foolish imaginations do not have to be evil in themselves. The problem is *they render our imaginations occupied and full, unable to receive God's vision.*

Only God-given vision brings us into the richness and blessings of God's purposes. Vain or foolish imaginations lead us astray from God's heart and purposes.

The key is what we put before our eyes - the pictures, images and imaginings that consume us. We will find that whatever we fill our minds and eyes with will become the imaginations of our heart.

Even as Christians we can let our imaginations be consumed with vain and foolish things that lead to vain imaginations and a lack of vision for our life.

I learned this lesson in my own life.

As a young man, I allowed myself to be consumed with surfing, to surround myself with surfing pictures and surfing videos. I wore surfer clothes, and had surfer friends who talked only of surfing. I had no God-given vision, but only a heart full of vain imaginations.

When I closed my eyes I saw waves. When I looked at a hillside, it looked like a wave to me. I thought and dreamed about surfing all the time. I tried to imagine ways to get out of my responsibilities so I could go surfing. It filled my imagination and gave direction to my life.

While there is certainly nothing wrong with surfing, I was in danger of living my life as nothing more than a surfer who had missed his God-given purpose and destiny.

This principle is true in every sphere of life.

A rich man once wrote, "Anyone can become fabulously wealthy if they will just eat, drink, talk, think, and sleep money." In other words, if they would fill their imaginations with thoughts and pictures of money, making it the core of their lives, they would develop the vision and imagination to make money. However, they would be following a vain imagination that in the end would cause them to lose their souls.

The Bible underscores the power of imagination to control our life.

This evil people, which refuse to hear my words, which walk in the imagination of their heart...

(Jeremiah 13:10, KJV)

The above verse shows the crux of my former problem with surfing: I was not giving sufficient place to God's Word in my life, but instead was filling my imagination with vanity. The creative power of my imagination was not being saturated with God's Word, so I was not able to receive vision. Instead, I was saturating it with something else.

The imagination can only focus on and hold so much. The Bible tells us that it is God's Word and listening prayer that must fill our imagination if we are to know godly success.

This book of the law shall not depart from your mouth, but you shall meditate on it day and night, so that you may be careful to do according to all that is written in it; for then you will make your way prosperous, and then you will have success.

(Joshua 1:8)

Meditating and giving careful attention to God's Word, and His great deeds, produces great benefit. Notice the promises given to those who fill their imaginations and hearts with the Word of God.

But his delight is in the law of the LORD, And in His law he meditates day and night. He will be like a tree firmly planted by streams of

*water, Which yields its fruit in its season And its leaf does not wither;
And in whatever he does, he prospers.*

(Psalm 1:2-3)

Delighting yourself in your heavenly Father's Word and meditating on His great deeds makes your imagination come alive!

Meditation upon God's great deeds and upon His Word is the creative womb where vision is birthed, where divine solutions and visions are given to us.

As we meditate on the biblical stories of how God moved with power and creativity to solve past crises, we become able to picture Him solving today's crises with the same power. As we meditate on His laws and precepts, we come to understand what went wrong and how to correct it. Creative solutions begin to come into our mind and spirit. As we meditate on His promises, our faith and courage are ignited to believe that God could use us. Through it all God begins to speak to us.

Gradually, vision begins to form deep within us, to take shape and gain substance, until it becomes clear and full-color, igniting faith within us, causing us to be stretched to God's proportions.

Great dreams are painted in our imaginations as we meditate upon God's Word. Our imaginations become the place where God paints vision. As we look at the problems that surround us in this day, we must do so with sanctified imaginations - imaginations that are meditating on God's Word and the great acts God has done in the past.

A Vision for Youth

This is the way, for instance, that Youth Venture - our church outreach to the community youth - began. Because we were greatly troubled over the conditions of our public schools, a number of our church members had run for various seats on local school boards in the November, 1991, elections. In the previous election cycle, a number of outspoken Christians had been elected, and there was a real opportunity to overthrow the status quo educational establishment and bring in much-needed change (which everyone says they want).

Our candidates were excellent, so none of us could have possibly been prepared for the hostility we would face from the national educational establishment. With total disregard for truth, they engineered a campaign of deliberate distortion and misrepresentation. Even more bizarre, these local school board elections received regular national coverage from the major news outlets. Imagine attending a candidates' debate for a small, suburban elementary school board race (i.e., La Mesa), and seeing *CBS Evening News,* the *Washington Post, Time* magazine, the *Los Angeles Times,* the *New York Times,* the *McNeil Lehrer Report* and the *New Yorker* magazine, among others, all covering the race (acting on a tip from the National Education Association), warning the nation of these "dangerous people" and their "secret agenda" to subvert democracy.

It was painful to watch our four candidates (all running for separate school boards) treated in this unfair way. Two of them were my wife's brothers. None of our candidates were able to overcome the nationally-aired misinformation campaign, and all lost. Certainly, it was disconcerting to be at the center of all this and it was discouraging to anyone wanting to help the younger generation.

However, when Jesus is your boss, you cannot grow disheartened. The word *defeat* is certainly not in God's vocabulary - except in regards to the enemy. You simply wait on God and His Word.

It is my practice to read my Bible, pray and meditate in the church sanctuary early in the morning. The morning after the above-mentioned candidate forum, as I studied, worshipped and waited on God in the sanctuary, God spoke to my heart through Isaiah 42:1-4. Within moments, He painted a broad vision in my imagination for what is now Youth Venture. Although it took months to clarify all the aspects, it was in those minutes as God gave the vision that Youth Venture was created. It was that vision that carried me through the difficult months of struggle to see the vision to fulfillment. Now, more than fifteen years later, Youth Venture, along with Higher Ground Clubs, has touched many thousands of young lives and has proven to be a vision that only God could have given or accomplished.

MEDITATE ON HIM AND HIS DEEDS

In Psalm 77, the writer is in the middle of a very difficult situation, where victory seems far from him. Notice this man's strategy in the middle of this difficult and dangerous situation.

> *...I will remember Your wonders of old. I will meditate on all Your work And muse on Your deeds.*
>
> (Psalm 77:11-12)

He understood what to do to face his present challenge. He would meditate and muse on God's great works and deeds. He knew that as he did so, his imagination would be filled with creative and encouraging power, and he would be a candidate to receive the vision for the hour.

The word *muse* is defined as ""a state of deep thought or dreamy abstraction." It is like a state of creative imagination, almost sanctified daydreaming. It is the process by which God begins to paint vision in our imaginations as we meditate upon the great needs of our day, and the great God who can do all things.

Too often, after a disappointment or failure, we focus on the failure or disappointment. But the psalmist understood that God was not defeated. Like the psalmist, we too must meditate on God and His Word at such times. Doing so is an act of worship that greatly honors and pleases God.

Imagination is a very powerful thing. Once we receive an imagination into our hearts, if we meditate upon it and muse on it, eventually it will come to fill our imaginations until, both consciously and unconsciously, we begin to express it in words and actions.

Soon it comes to dominate our lifestyles.

Finally, we begin to see the fulfillment of that which first began in our imaginations. That is the power of imagination. This powerful tool must be given to serve God.

OUR IMAGINATIONS CAN HURT US OR HELP US

Imagination can work for us or against us. A negative imagination can bring destruction into our lives.

In Numbers 13, Israel stands on the brink of the Promised Land. Moses, acting under God's directions, sends in twelve spies to spy out the land. These twelve men had all seen the plagues that God had worked upon the Egyptians, they had all passed through the Red Sea, and they had all seen the great manifestations of God on Mount Sinai when God gave Moses the Ten Commandments. Further, they all knew that this same God had promised to give them this land.

Nevertheless, they came back with very different reports from their scouting trip. Ten spies gave a negative report, and only two, Joshua and Caleb gave a good report.

Listen to the report of the ten spies.

...We are not able to go up against the people, for they are too strong for us...The land through which we have gone, in spying it out, is a land that devours its inhabitants; and all the people whom we saw in it are men of great size. There also we saw the Nephilim (the sons of Anak are part of the Nephilim); *and we became like grasshoppers in our own sight, and so we were in their sight.*

(Numbers 13:31-33)

Listen to their words: "*a land that devours its inhabitants*" and a people of "*great size*" before whom they appeared and felt like "*grasshoppers.*" Do you hear these spies letting their imaginations beginning to paint a picture for them? Do you hear the exaggeration? We might say that they were letting their imaginations get the best of them and defeat them. How different is the report by Caleb and Joshua!

…The land which we passed through to spy out is an exceedingly good land. If the LORD is pleased with us, then He will bring us into this land and give it to us - a land flowing with milk and honey. Only do not rebel against the LORD; and do not fear the people of the land, for they will be our prey…

(Numbers 14:7-9)

Notice that two very different imaginations are being nurtured in these verses. One imagination will lead to failure, defeat and shame.

The other will lead surely to faith, victory and honor.

Joshua and Caleb were painting a picture in their imaginations that would lead to obedience and faith. They said, *"They will be our prey,"* or as we might put it, "We will have them for breakfast." Their imaginations were receiving the vision.

We have the same choices available to us today. What do we see in our imaginations? Are our imaginations being fired by God's Word, or by circumstances and the unbelieving prattle of well-meaning friends and secular "experts"? Each of us has a promised land to take. God's promises extend to every area of our lives, our families, our future, our church and our community. We need to resist wrong thoughts and imaginations that are faith stealers and initiative killers.

13

The Kingdom Key of Submission: The Principle of Delegated Authority

Co-written by
David Hoffman and Mark Hoffman

> *Every person is to be in subjection to the governing authorities. For there is no authority except from God…for it is a minister of God to you for good.*
>
> (Romans 13:1, 4)

If one thing marks us as modern Americans, it is a distrust and hostility to authority.

Americans resist authority at every level.

Even as Christians, many of us struggle with the Church teachings concerning authority because we misunderstand them. We have been influenced by our culture's view of authority, and the idea of submission grates on us.

But Christians are given a deeper understanding and deeper wisdom than the world. Christians understand that submitting to authority is a key to open up God's superabundant Kingdom.

The above scripture calls all of us to willingly submit to authority because we understand that it is a ministry of God to us for our good.

God loves us and seeks to bring His blessings to us, and He instituted the Principle of Delegated Authority for that purpose.

The Bible everywhere assures us that God desires to share His wisdom, gifts, guidance and blessings with us. How does God deliver these to us?

One primary way is through authorities that He delegates over our lives. This is truly God's chain of supply into our lives. By this plan, God ensures that the blessings enrich us rather than spoil us since we have to maintain a respectful and submissive attitude to receive them - attitudes God desires and requires in His children if we are to succeed in His Creation.

We live in an ordered universe in which authority and submitting to authority are simply realities we must accept. A right understanding and relationship with authority is absolutely necessary if we are to advance in God's Kingdom, or in His world.

EVERYTHING HAS A HIERARCHY OF AUTHORITY

In the Godhead, there is a hierarchy even though there is equality. The Son only does the will of the Father (John 5:30), for it was the Father who sent Him (John 17:18). In the same way, Jesus sent the Holy Spirit (John 16:7), and the Holy Spirit will only speak what He hears (John 16:13). Even in the Godhead, where there is absolute equality, the principles of authority and submission are active.

Among the angels there is a hierarchy with authority and submission. We read of ranks of angels, for instance, the archangels, the cherubim and the seraphim.

There is a clear hierarchy in the Church, with elders and the five-fold offices (Ephesians 4:11-13). There is a clear hierarchy in society with government and various levels of authority that require our submission.

And finally, there is a clear hierarchy in the family unit, with children submitting to parents and the wife submitting to the husband (Ephesians 5:22-6:4).

Because authority and submission are such important parts of God's design and plan, we suffer great loss if we resist or ignore them.

HOW GOD USES AUTHORITIES IN OUR LIVES

We read, in the verse that began this chapter, that authorities are "a minister of God to you for your good." The Greek word translated minister here is the word *diakonos*, which means servant or attendant. It is the same word that is translated as deacon in several other places. In the New Testament, the deacon was given the responsibility of distributing food and goods to those in need within the church (Acts 6).

In the same way, the primary purpose of authority is to serve as a channel of God's blessing and supply to us. Beginning from our birth, God supplies us through those that He puts over us. In our early years, our parents feed and clothe us, and teach us how to avoid hazards and learn skills. Then we submit to teachers who teach us, employers who enrich us, police who protect us and church leaders who bring us knowledge and wisdom of God's will and ways. (This list could be greatly extended.)

This means that *if we refuse to submit to the authorities God has placed over us, we cut off the protection and supply God wants to give us.* The child who ignores his teacher will not learn. The teen who rebels against her parents and sneaks around behind their backs will forfeit the wisdom and protection God would bring her through them. She will one day wake up in a very bad place, wondering why God let awful things happen to her. The truth is that she stepped out from under God's channel of guidance and protection.

The employee who disrespects and poorly serves his employer will soon find that he has undercut God's source of supply. As he stands in the unemployment line, he may complain bitterly to God that he has no money, yet the blessing from God was lost because the messenger from God was disrespected.

The Kingdom Key of Submission may be stated in this way: **When we submit to the authorities God has put in our lives, we open the supply lines from heaven. When we rebel against those authorities, we hinder God's supply from coming to us.**

This principle remains true, even though the authority may be very flawed.

Many people struggle with accepting this point.

Although they trust God, they have little or no confidence in the authority over them, and so they despise or resist it. However, we must be able to look beyond the authority figure and see God Himself as the source of our supply, standing behind that authority. If our attitude to authority is right, God will still be faithful to bring us what we need. Often He will even use those very same problem authorities to supply us in spite of themselves.

The king's heart is like channels of water in the hand of the LORD;
He turns it wherever He wishes.

(Proverbs 21:1)

Here we see that the Lord is the true power behind the authority (in this case, the king). The king is merely the servant of the Lord to accomplish His will. Therefore, the Lord can cause any authority to accomplish His will to benefit those who are trusting in God.

THE SPIRIT OF SUBMISSION

When we understand the Kingdom Key of Submission, we are then ready to fully embrace the spirit of submission.

Many people think they are submitting simply because they are not disobeying. They believe that because they are not overtly disobeying any direct commands or directions, they are fulfilling the biblical injunction to submit.

The spirit of submission is much more than avoiding direct disobedience!

It is a positive action as well.

It is an attitude that seeks out the advice and blessing of the authority, recognizing that God will bring wisdom and supply to us through God's delegated authorities, *despite* their weaknesses.

Many people have a negative view of authority, distrusting and avoiding it. In many cases, the subordinate will try to let the one in authority know as little as possible about what they are doing. In this way, they reason, the authority will not be able to hurt them. However, the reverse is also true...the authority will not be able to help them.

People distrust authority for many reasons. They may have been hurt once by an authority they have never fully forgiven, or perhaps they are operating in the sinful pride of their human hearts. If they are Christians, they may even obey whatever orders come to them, but they do not invite the authority into their affairs. That way, the authority can only give a minimum of direction to be "obeyed."

This is a legalistic misunderstanding of authority, and ultimately misses much of God's guidance and supply.

SATAN SEEKS TO UNDERMINE AUTHORITY

One of Satan's greatest weapons to divide and neutralize a local assembly is for Christians to begin to question all levels of spiritual authority in the church and the family.

Satan's goal is to get members of local congregations to question its leaders' integrity, ability and motives. The devil's intent is to destroy the church's supply lines from God, destroy their unity, and hamper their ability to make an impact in their community.

Usually this rebelliousness is clothed with great justification, concern and religiosity. It sounds as if the individuals or group (those questioning church leadership) are really concerned for the welfare of the church. But, in reality, the aim of the spirit behind them is to divide and destroy what the Lord Jesus has been doing.

Finding fault with leadership in any Christian congregation is not difficult because we all have faults and all are sinners.

Always remember that imperfect authorities in our lives serve as tests to reveal whether rebellion or submissiveness rules in our hearts. Maintaining a submissive attitude with flawed authorities is an act of worship that is greatly appreciated by God. God rewards us when we are submissive for His sake.

> *Servants, be submissive to your masters with all respect, not only to those who are good and gentle, but also to those who are unreasonable. For this finds favor, if for the sake of conscience toward God a person bears up under sorrows when suffering unjustly.*
>
> (1 Peter 2:18-19)

In the family, if the authority structure that God has set up is deliberately undermined or abdicated, all members of that family suffer the consequences. The children exhibit rebellion, insecurities, anger, lack of discipline and so on, and the husband and wife experience relationship problems because they step outside of God's created will for their lives. Certainly this has been the legacy of the modern philosophies that are trying to redefine in unbiblical ways the roles between husbands, wives and their children.

GOD DELEGATES HIS AUTHORITY

A study of the Bible will show that God delegates His authority to human representatives.

It is necessary for family members and church members to submit themselves to the authority structure of the church and family so that the church grows united in its effectiveness for the Gospel of Jesus Christ.

Even a quick study of the New Testament reveals how Jesus operates His authority through the Church. After defeating Satan at the cross and being raised to the right hand of the Father, Jesus assumed His position of having all authority. We read that God:

> *...seated Him at His right hand in the heavenly places, far above all rule and authority and power and dominion, and every name that is named, not only in this age but also in the one to come. And He put all things in subjection under His feet, and gave Him as head over all things to the church, which is His body, the fullness of Him who fills all in all.*
>
> (Ephesians 1:20-23)

The Church carries Jesus' authority and power. Jesus set up an administration to dispense His authority through the Church. In this same chapter, we read that God's plan was to set up:

> *...an administration suitable to the fullness of the times, that is, the summing up of all things in Christ...*
>
> (Ephesians 1:10)

God's plan was to sum up everything in Christ. The Greek word for "sum up" is a derivative of the word *kephale*, which translates as "head." God wants to bring everything under the headship of Christ. His plan to do this is to set up an *"administration."*

The Greek word translated *administration* is the word *oikonomia* which has the meaning of "administration, management, economy or dispensation."

It is the system by which Jesus will distribute His wisdom, riches, protection and help to the world.

This administration is the Church.

Every president, upon election, begins to set up his administration. It is his first order of business. He knows that he can't deliver his campaign promises without a good administration. He knows that he can't rule without an administration. Before he does anything else, he begins to appoint people to his cabinet posts to head up his administration.

Jesus Christ did the same thing. As soon as He ascended to His Father's right side, He began to set up His administration.

"WHEN HE ASCENDED ON HIGH, HE LED CAPTIVE A HOST OF CAPTIVES, AND HE GAVE GIFTS TO MEN." And He gave some as apostles, and some as prophets, and some as evangelists, and some as pastors and teachers, for the equipping of the saints for the work of service, to the building up of the body of Christ.

(Ephesians 4:8, 11-12)

Jesus began to set up His administration by giving gifts of divinely-chosen and anointed men to serve as officers in His administration. These five offices that Christ set in the Church are the chief stewards of God's mercy to the Church to bring it to wholeness and maturity. If their authority is not received, then the Christian will suffer a serious supply shortage. These men are called and supernaturally gifted to stand in these offices. This is Jesus' plan to supply His saints and build His Church. That is why the Bible instructs us:

Obey your leaders and submit to them, for they keep watch over your souls as those who will give an account. Let them do this with joy and not with grief, for this would be unprofitable for you.

(Hebrews 13:17)

The reason to submit to leadership is for your profit. When we refuse to submit, it proves *"unprofitable"* to us.

Why would some in the body of Christ be responsible for others? Only because they have been supernaturally gifted with special grace and enablement. They are responsible to use this gifting to serve and watch out for the others.

The other side of this, however, is that people must respect and submit to this gift and call. When through ignorance or pride we fear or resist duly-ordained Church leadership, we frustrate Jesus' plan and hinder His grace from coming into our lives.

It is easy to see that God has set up delegated authority in the New Testament.

In Titus 1:5-9 we see the mandate to appoint elders in every place and also a list of their qualifications. In 1 Timothy 3:1-13 we see a similar list for elders or overseers, and also an additional list for deacons and deaconesses. As we have seen, we are called to be in submission to such leaders.

Why has God put delegated authority in the midst of His Church? The answer is that He did it to build up the Church and bring it into the purposes of God.

In Ephesians 5:22-23, God tells the wife to be subject to her husband. Why? Because God has given the husband His delegated authority. When a wife submits to her husband, she submits to the spiritual authority resting on him from God - not the man himself. This opens up a channel of supply from God Himself.

This doesn't mean a wife must always agree with her husband - only that she recognize and submit to the authority given to him from God. That is why, at the end of Ephesians 5:33 (NKV), Paul says, *"Let the wife see that she respects her husband."*

In Colossians 3:20, Paul tells children to *"be obedient to your parents in all things."*

It is easy to see from the Bible that the Lord wants us not only to be submissive to His *direct* authority, but also His *delegated* authority.

THE PRINCIPLE OF APPEAL

Concerning delegated authority, the questions often asked are, "What if they're wrong?" "What if their actions are unfair or unjust?" "What should I do if I disagree with delegated authority?"

If there is disagreement, never go to your peers and grumble and discredit the authority. This can do great damage to all involved, and reveals a rebellious spirit. Instead, go to the delegated authority with your concerns. Many times, as you go to them with godly respect and submission, God will respond by giving them the wisdom and grace to receive what you are saying. As you do, everyone will benefit from your faithfulness.

"But what do I do if they still won't listen to me?"

Then you must understand the principle of appeal.

No authority is autonomous - all authority is derived from a higher source.

For example, a sergeant only has authority as he is in submission to his superiors. A person can only have authority as he or she is under authority. Jesus praised a Roman centurion for understanding this principle. The centurion recognized that both Jesus' authority and his authority came from being under authority.

The centurion recognized that his authority, as well as Jesus' authority, was only possible because each was rightly submitted to authority. Just as he was submitted to Caesar and his delegates, so Jesus was yielded to God, His Father. He understood that Jesus' authority to heal all diseases proved that He was a faithful and submitted representative of God. For this reason he was unworthy to have Jesus under his roof.

...Lord, I am not worthy for You to come under my roof, but just say the word, and my servant will be healed. For I also am a man under authority, with soldiers under me; and I say to this one "Go!" and he goes, and to another "Come!" and he comes...

(Matthew 8:8-9)

Since all authorities are themselves under authority, there is always a higher authority to whom to appeal in order to protect against cruel or unjust treatment. Appeal rather than rebellion is the godly course to follow.

The appeal process is illustrated in our legal system. If you believe you have been mistreated by the lower court, you are not permitted to disobey or show disrespect for that court or judge, but you are free to file an appeal with a higher court. The higher court can overthrow the decision of the lower court.

Many wives are afraid to embrace the biblical teaching on submission within the home because they are afraid of being victimized. I have even heard it taught that, according to the Bible, if a man beats his wife that she should submit to it.

Nonsense!

This is a gross distortion of the Bible's teaching on submission.

A husband is not an autonomous authority! He too is under authority. He is under the authority of the state, and, if he is a Christian, he is under the authority of the Church. If he beats his wife, he is violating the authority of the state and the authority of the Church. He has no authority granted him to hit his wife. The wife is right and justified to appeal to the higher authorities for protection. She should call the police and their pastor. She is still under submission because she is submitting to the higher authorities.

Appeal to a higher authority is an avenue that God has granted all of His children.

Even the great apostle Paul exercised this right. Paul, when he felt he could not get justice from the local Procurator Festus, appealed to Caesar and was sent to Rome for trial (Acts 25:10-11). Remember, God is the final authority from whom all other authority is derived. Appealing to a higher authority is always done with a submissive and respectful spirit because God is the ultimate source of all authority.

An authority who rejects and rebels against those above him loses his authority and must no longer be submitted to, at least in the area of his or her rebellion. We are responsible to obey the higher authorities. That is why wives and children are not to submit to the heads of their families when it involves breaking the law.

In the New Testament, believers disobeyed the authorities when the Jewish leaders told Peter and John to stop preaching about Jesus (a command against God's divine law). They told them; "We must obey God rather than man" (Acts 4:19-20).

Finally, even if all human authorities involved are wrong or unjust, we always have a final appeal to God. We must follow the example of our Lord who suffered from unjust treatment by authorities.

For you have been called for this purpose, since Christ also suffered for you, leaving you an example for you to follow in His steps, WHO COMMITTED NO SIN, NOR WAS ANY DECEIT FOUND IN HIS MOUTH; and while being reviled, He did not revile in return...but kept entrusting Himself to Him who judges righteously.
(1 Peter 2:21-23)

GOD REQUIRES THAT WE SUBMIT TO AUTHORITY

If God has entrusted His authority to men/women, then we need to be submissive to that authority. Since God has instituted His delegated authority in the Church and the family, He is bound by His honor to maintain that authority and to defend it. And He will!

Many profess to know God, profess obedience, but know nothing of obeying and being submissive to delegated authority in the Church as well as in the family. Since God has put His delegated authority in the Church family, we must learn to submit to this authority, otherwise we find ourselves in rebellion against God.

This is a sobering thought.

An example of this principle is found in the life of Moses and the nation of Israel. The Israelites, who were traveling through the wilderness, were complaining about and threatening the leadership of Moses (God's appointed man) because they were displeased with their circumstances and felt their lives were in danger. Moses told them that their grumbling and insubordination against him was really against God.

... for the LORD hears your grumblings which you grumble against Him. And what are we? Your grumblings are not against us but against the LORD.

(Exodus 16:8)

Look how God reacts to rebellion against delegated authority:

Now Korah the son of Izhar, the son of Kohath, the son of Levi, with Dathan and Abiram, the sons of Eliab, and On the son of Peleth, sons of Reuben, took action, and they rose up before Moses, together with some of the sons of Israel, two hundred and fifty leaders of the congregation, chosen in the assembly, men of renown. They assembled together against Moses and Aaron, and said to them, "You have gone far enough, for all the congregation are holy, every one of them, and the LORD is in their midst; so why do you exalt yourselves above the assembly of the LORD?"

(Numbers 16:1-3)

Notice this rebellion was brought about by reason and logical think-ing. "You're no better than us, you take too much authority upon yourself; it would be safer if the authority was divided up." The people thought they were opposing Moses and Aaron, when, in effect, they were rebelling against God!

What was God's response to this rebellion? We read of it a little later in the same chapter.

And the earth opened its mouth and swallowed them up, and their households, and all the men who belonged to Korah with their posses-sions. So they and all that belonged to them went down alive to Sheol; and the earth closed over them, and they perished from the midst of the assembly. All Israel who were around them fled at their outcry, for they said," The earth may swallow us up!" Fire also came forth from the LORD and consumed the two hundred and fifty men who were offer-ing the incense.

(Numbers 16:32-35)

Even after all this, the people did not learn their lesson. The very next day, some people rose up against Moses. A true leader, Moses recognized the danger that they were putting themselves in and had Aaron, the priest, begin to pray for them.

While Aaron was interceding before God to have mercy upon His rebel-lious people, a plague was sent by the Lord. Before it was over, 14,700 Israelites had died (Numbers 16:41-45). Disregarding and disrespecting God's delegated authorities in the family, church or government is serious and always results in judgment and suffering.

Any parent who allows their children to disregard or disrespect their authority in any way is inviting sorrows into their child's life. The Bible makes it clear that we represent both God's provision and His authority over our children. He offers His protection, guidance and blessing to children through their parents. However, if a child rejects his parents' authority then he is, in essence, rejecting God. He will, therefore, fall under a curse.

Cursed is he who dishonors his father or mother...
(Deuteronomy 27:16)

The eye that mocks a father And scorns a mother, The ravens of the valley will pick it out, And the young eagles will eat it.
(Proverbs 30:17)

So much of the devastation we see among our youth in regards to addiction, suicide, violence, teen pregnancy and unhappiness is rooted in the failure of their parents to teach them respect and submission to authority. Because of humanistic ideas, many parents are unwilling to control their children (including spanking if necessary) and thereby enforce obedience. Believe me, spanking is not child abuse; rather, allowing your children to disregard and disobey you is the true child abuse. It brings with it a lifetime of suffering and unhappiness.

RECOGNIZING SPIRITUAL AUTHORITY

Those who fear God recognize and respect God's authority as it rests on people. In Acts 9, we find Paul meeting the Lord, the supreme authority, on the road to Damascus. Three days later, Paul, a high Jewish official, "a Hebrew of Hebrews," submits himself to Ananias, a little-known man of Damascus.

Paul never criticized Ananias, but recognized him as the delegated authority of God. So, Paul submitted himself.

King David was another great hero of the Bible who feared God and respected His delegated authorities, even though they were sinful and flawed. This is especially evident in his dealing with King Saul, even when Saul pursued him to kill him.

He came to the sheepfolds on the way, where there was a cave; and Saul went in to relieve himself. Now David and his men were sitting in the inner recesses of the cave. The men of David said to him, "Behold, this is the day of which the LORD said to you, 'Behold; I am about to give

157

your enemy into your hand, and you shall do to him as it seems good to you.'" Then David arose and cut off the edge of Saul's robe secretly. It came about afterward that David's conscience bothered him because he had cut off the edge of Saul's robe. So he said to his men, "Far be it from me because of the LORD that I should do this thing to my lord, the LORD'S anointed, to stretch out my hand against him, since he is the LORD'S anointed." David persuaded his men with these words and did not allow them to rise up against Saul. And Saul arose, left the cave, and went on his way.

(1 Samuel 24:3-7)

David had another chance to kill Saul (1 Samuel 26:7-11), but refused to lift his hand against God's anointed.

King David understood authority. This was one of the reasons God called him a man after His own heart.

If anyone wishes to serve God - to do great things for God - he or she must first learn to be subject to God's delegated authority in the Church and family.

If David had killed King Saul and took the kingdom for himself, he would have been as weak as Saul because he would have opened himself up to a rebellious spirit.

Remember, God has placed authority in the family, society and Church to bless and supply you. We cannot honor God if we dishonor those to whom He has delegated some of His authority. Authority given over us is a blessing, not a curse. It is God's servant to bring His riches and blessings into our life.

14

The Kingdom Key of Displacement

...the stone that struck the statue became a great mountain and filled the whole earth.

(Daniel 2:35)

It is the nature of our world that one thing is displaced by another.

Darkness will fill a room until a door from a lighted hallway is opened, then light floods into the room and displaces the darkness. A glass is filled with air until water is poured into it and the air is displaced. One political party holds tightly to power until it is displaced by another.

In the nature of things, that which is will remain until it is displaced by something else. Where can you observe anything simply abandoning its place and leaving an empty nothingness?

It is against the laws of nature.

Consider the well-known saying that you probably first learned from your high school science teacher: "Nature abhors (hates) a vacuum." This means that something will always rush in to fill a void, and that something of greater density or energy will displace something of lesser density or energy.

Nature abhors a vacuum. This simple statement of general truth applies in the physical world, and also in the spiritual, social and moral realms as well.

One thing can only be permanently driven out by something greater. You cannot drive out something with nothing. The principle of displacement may be stated this way:

That which is will remain until it is challenged by something greater, and then it must give place to the greater.

It is not enough to find fault with a reigning system. If all you do is criticize or find fault, you will never accomplish real change in yourself or anyone else. You will never see true change in your church, government or education system by merely criticizing or finding fault. You must present a new and superior alternative. Harmful things will not be driven out permanently unless there is something greater, something with more truth, energy and vitality, to take its place.

Jesus illustrated this principle.

Now when an unclean spirit goes out of a man, it passes through waterless places seeking rest, and does not find it. Then it says, "I will return to my house from which I came"; and when it comes, it finds it unoccupied, swept, and put in order. Then it goes and takes along with it seven other spirits more wicked than itself, and they go in and live there; and the last state of that man becomes worse than the first. That is the way it will also be with this evil generation.

(Matthew 12:43-45)

Sin, bad habits, demons, unjust systems, deceptive philosophies or wrong beliefs cannot be defeated unless they are replaced with something else! Otherwise, they will simply return again and again ("nature abhors a vacuum"). We must not seek merely to attack unrighteousness, but to build righteous things to take their place.

Displacement is the tool God has given His children to remove unrighteousness. In fact, it is our very nature to dispossess and displace. Jesus Himself said: *"You are the light of the world"* (Matthew 5:14).

There is nothing more obviously true about light than that it displaces darkness. Wherever light shines, darkness retreats and recedes. Darkness can only exist in the absence of light. Note that Jesus did not say "In some ways you are like light." He said very simply, "You are light." By our very nature as born-again, Spirit-filled children of God, it is in our very nature to dispossess and displace darkness.

IF YOU BUILD IT THEY WILL COME

The greatest advances of God's people come not when they criticize and point out the weaknesses of other systems, but when they put their energy on building the Kingdom of God.

This was the strategy of the early Church. Rather than focus on critiquing the religious and civil authorities, they set about to build a new system and a whole new community. Jesus had taught them that new wine required new wineskins (Matthew 9:17).

They set out to displace the sinful ideas, beliefs, structures and practices of the Jewish and Roman societies by replacing them with a new vision and a new message. They boldly proclaimed the new teaching of Jesus everywhere with boldness.

And daily in the temple, and in every house, they ceased not to teach and preach Jesus Christ.

(Acts 5:42, KJV)

They were so effective that the Jewish authorities accused the apostles by saying: *"You have filled Jerusalem with your teaching"* (Acts 5:28). They so filled Jerusalem with this teaching in the power of the Holy Spirit that their city began changing.

The word of God kept on spreading; and the number of the disciples continued to increase greatly in Jerusalem, and a great many of the priests were becoming obedient to the faith.

(Acts 6:7)

With these new converts, they began to build new communities where they practiced a new ethic of love (Acts 2:42-47). But the vision that Jesus had given them went far beyond Jerusalem, to encompass the whole world. These Christian leaders set out to fill the whole known world with the glorious teaching of Jesus Christ.

They continued this until they had so filled the ancient world with the truth about Jesus, the forgiveness of sins, love and reconciliation that the world began to change. Old ideas, old customs and old institutions gradually began to be abandoned and replaced. City leaders of the city of Thessalonica, who had a vested interest in preserving the old status quo, cried in alarm when Paul and his companions began to minister in their city;

These who have turned the world upside down have come here too.

(Acts 17:6, NKJ)

But nothing could stop the advance of the light into darkness. In time, even the abominations of pagan Rome, as well as their pantheon of false gods, began to be abandoned.

By the end of the second century the influential church leader Tertullian would write in his book, *Apologeticum: An Impassioned Defense*, addressing the pagan Roman ruling class, "We (Christians) have filled everything you have, cities, tenements, forts towns, exchanges, yes, and army camps, tribes, palace, senate, forum. All we have left you is the (pagan) temples" (*Apologeticum* 37:4-5).

By 391 A.D., Christianity had so displaced those systems that Emperor Theodosius declared Christianity to be the official religion of the Roman Empire. However, this proved to be a great setback to Christianity's future. You see, as long as the Christians kept their focus on building the Kingdom of God, they displaced the sinful and unjust systems and ideas of the ancient Roman society. However, once they came to have a preferred place in Roman society, they soon became enamored with worldly power and earthly kingdoms and gradually lost sight of the Kingdom of God.

This is not to say that Christians should not speak out prophetically in the public square or be involved in the systems of this world (like politics and state-run education).

Far from it! There is a great need for Christians in all realms. We must be salt and light in every area. Great harm comes when Christians abandon their responsibilities as citizens. How different America would be if all Christians simply voted (typically only about one third of Christians who are eligible to register and vote actually do. If ninety percent voted, we would control every election). Likewise, Christians must exercise influence in every sphere of our society.

For instance, several of our church members have run for and won seats on our local city council and local school boards. We also operate on-site after-school Bible clubs at twenty-four area public school campuses (but more important is the fact that we have begun and operate two Christian schools!) Likewise we have been very active in political action and voter registration, and have worked effectively to influence legislation (but more importantly we have involved 1,100 people in our Prayer Society).

The secular political and educational realms are important, but they are not our first place. Our first place is to follow Jesus in building the Kingdom of God. It is good and necessary for Christians to become involved in the school boards of our public schools, but it is not our highest calling and in the end it will be a losing strategy. It is better when we create new, effective and godly forms of educating the young.

It is good when Christians volunteer to help out in government-sponsored low-income housing projects, but it is even better when Christians develop new biblical ways of teaching the poor God's laws of prosperity. As Christians, we must remember that Jesus does not just want us to take part in the world's business, He intends for us to take over!

Our calling as disciples of Jesus is not to engage in some defensive, running skirmish against the advance of the forces of Satan. Too often we take potshots at the advancing enemy instead of following God-ordained, God-inspired leadership into building the Kingdom of God.

God is not calling us to put the bulk of our energy into criticizing the humanist solutions or tinkering with or improving their socialist programs. He is calling us to replace them with biblical solutions.

Instead, Christians should be leading with positive solutions.

Christians today are more known for what they are against. Unsaved people know that we are AGAINST abortion, feminism, socialism, humanism, the gay agenda and New Age spiritualism.

The world wonders if we are FOR anything. They wonder why, if we have no answers of our own to confront the great social problems of our day, we oppose all those who claim that they do have the answers. This is part of the reason we are scorned by the media and the intellectual community.

We should have the answers to resolve the great problems of our culture. We are, after all, the salt of the earth. Jesus is yearning to give His people the strategies and plans to heal our society and deliver people from destruction and the power of sin. Jesus wants to give us the ideas, strategies and structures that are so good that they displace all the counterfeit solutions of the humanists, socialists and hedonists.

Jesus wants to install His servants in the seats of spiritual, political and cultural influence over this culture – many of which are presently under the influence of demonic strongholds and principalities. Jesus has given us the authority to displace them and take our place as those who live out the good news of the reign of Jesus until the earth is *"full of the knowledge of the LORD As the waters cover the sea"* (Isaiah 11:9).

In fact, God promises to do this very thing. God operates by the Principle of Displacement to bring righteousness and peace to His world.

*For evildoers will be cut off, But those who wait for the LORD, they will inherit the land. Yet little while and the wicked man will be no more; **And you will look carefully for his place and he will not be there. But the humble will inherit the land**...*

(Psalm 37:9-11)

*The wicked is a ransom for the righteous, **And the treacherous is in the place of the upright**.*

(Proverbs 21:18)

...the wealth of the sinner is stored up for the righteous.

(Proverbs 13:22)

God's desire is to replace the unrighteous with the righteous. Jesus said that it was the meek (those who have humbled themselves under God's hand), not the ungodly, who would inherit the land (Matthew 5:5, KJV). This is God's plan and promise.

The truth is that sin does not prosper. It is judged by God, and those who practice lawlessness sooner or later (usually sooner) are in for a great fall. We see this all around us in the world of politics, entertainment and even business. However, the void will soon be filled by another. If no one righteous is ready to step in, then it will be another lawless person who will fill the void, only to be judged and fall and then to be replaced by another...and so it goes on and on. God wants us to understand the law of displacement and allow Him to promote us to fill the places of influence and dominion.

This has been exactly our experience! Our church was opposed by many powerful people in local educational and political circles. They did whatever was possible to frustrate what we believed God had called us to do. In every single case, except one, those people are all gone now and in many cases have been replaced by people in our church or our friends. In the case of the one who still remains, he has stopped all opposition and now courts our friendship (the exciting story of how this happened is told in my book *On Earth as It Is in Heaven*).

Let us look at the law of displacement on three levels: First, displacement in the heavenlies; second, displacement in earthly governments and philosophies; and third, displacement within a person.

DISPLACEMENT IN THE HEAVENLY PLACES

The Bible teaches that spiritual beings exercise great influence over the lives of men, societies and the whole world from positions of power and authority in a heavenly realm.

> *For our struggle is not against flesh and blood, but against the rulers* (principalities - KJV), *against the powers, against the world forces of this darkness, against the spiritual forces of wickedness in the heavenly places.*
>
> (Ephesians 6:12)

> *So that the manifold wisdom of God might now be made known through the church to the rulers* (principalities, KJV) *and authorities in the heavenly places.*
>
> (Ephesians 3:10)

These verses (and others) describe a demonic hierarchy of evil spirit beings through which Satan influences and afflicts the world. They are probably fallen angels, like Satan himself, who rebelled along with him. The heavenly places or realms that are spoken of here are not the highest heaven where God dwells, but some intermediate spiritual realm. From this vantage point, evil spirits exercise great power and influence.

As Christians, we must war against these spirits if we are to see our culture set free from their domination. Even our loved ones for whom we pray are greatly hindered from coming to Christ by these powerful agents.

Principalities and powers work to strengthen racial and cultural pride and to promote strife, lust, addictions and violence as well as religious and spiritual deception. Successful evangelism of a city or region depends on overcoming such dark powers. But how are such powers defeated? The Book of Revelation gives us an answer.

And there was war in heaven, Michael and his angels waging war with the dragon. The dragon and his angels waged war, and they were not strong enough, and there was no longer a place found for them in heaven. And the great dragon was thrown down, the serpent of old who is called the devil and Satan, who deceives the whole world...

(Revelation 12:7-9)

Here is a very clear picture of the principle of displacement in action. Satan and demonic power are permanently displaced from the heavenly realm by superior force, and there is no longer any place left for them.

Note that this displacement of Satan from the heavenly realms was related to the successful spiritual warfare of God's people here on earth. The very next verse says,

Then I heard a loud voice in heaven, saying, "Now the salvation, and the power, and the kingdom of our God and the authority of His Christ have come, for the accuser of our brethren has been thrown down, he who accuses them before our God day and night." And they overcame him because of the blood of the Lamb and because of the word of their testimony, and they did not love their life even when faced with death.

(Revelation 12:10-11)

As God's people resisted the devil through their faith in the blood of Jesus, by their words of testimony and willingness to be faithful to Jesus even to the point of facing death, they overcame Satan and he was displaced from the heavenly realms.

The heavenly realms are obviously a strategic place of great power, influence and advantage. We know this because the devil, after having been displaced from there, realizes *"that he has only a short time"* (Revelation 12:12).

As we come into agreement and submission to the power of Christ's blood, and confess agreement with His Word in our testimony and actions, Satan and his hierarchy find themselves displaced. It is the cooperation of the Church here on earth with our heavenly Commander that gives victory. As we pray Spirit-led prayers, offer Spirit-inspired testimony, and do Spirit-inspired works of righteousness, we destroy the hold of darkness on earth. Falsehood, deception, hatred and corruption are overcome here on earth and, at the same time, the power of God displaces Satan's hold in the heavenlies.

Corresponding to that displacement, we will see an even greater release upon the earth of evangelism, healing and the advance of the Church.

Here, in the East County of San Diego, we are seeing a powerful illustration of this dynamic. Over twenty years ago, a number of pastors gathered together, at the invitation of my good friend George Runyan of City Church ministries, to begin praying for our city. The Church in San Diego had always been known for its lack of cooperation and unity. A strong spirit of competition and independence had always marked the Church here. In recent years, several world-famous evangelists had stated that they would not return here because the churches could not cooperate for a large crusade. In fact, as early as 1906, Frank Bartleman, one of the prime figures in the Pentecostal revival, cut short a planned two-week crusade in San Diego due to lack of cooperation between the churches.

Because of this traditional lack of unity, both the Pentecostal and Charismatic revivals as well as the later Jesus movement were greatly hindered here. They did not have the impact in San Diego that they did in many other parts of the country.

To my knowledge, until recently, there had never been a significant citywide work of God in San Diego's history.

When pastors from the East County realized what was going on in our town, we decided to gather together to pray.

The growth of this prayer group started off slowly. But gradually more pastors, desperate to see the hand of God move in their community, grew in their commitment to each other and to prayer.

Week in and week out we gathered to pray.

Often, we were hard-pressed to see much effect at all from our praying. But gradually, signs began to emerge.

We began to share finances when needed.

Pastors joined together with hammers and saws to build one of the churches.

We began to hold multi-church prayer meetings.

On a number of occasions, several hundred of our people joined in intercession on a mountain overlooking our city.

More pastors joined the prayer meetings. Eventually, we discovered that several other prayer groups had started across the county, inspired by what was happening in East County. (Today there are about 250 pastors who meet for prayer in over a dozen groups across our county.)

As we began to come into unity and agreement with our Head who is in heaven, expressed love and cooperation with one another, and united in intercession, demonic principalities and powers in the heavens began to be displaced!

Amazing breakthroughs came to our citywide Church which for so long had been known for division and apathy. We saw astonishing results.

● San Diego held the largest Life Chain ever held by any city. Twenty-seven thousand Christians lined the streets holding pro-life signs.

● San Diego churches and Christians united to elect so many Christian candidates to local offices (particularly in the East County) that it attracted national attention. Literally, every major television and print news media descended on the East County for months to report on this "miracle." Political consultants and political power brokers nationwide were thrown into an absolute panic.

● San Diego held the largest ever, first-time March for Jesus. Over 25,000 Christians marched in the parade. No city in the world had ever had as large a first-time turn out.

● Tens of thousands of Christian men filled the San Diego Qualcomm stadium for a very successful Promise Keepers Conference.

● Many other successful citywide crusades and meetings have been held including a four-day Billy Graham Crusade which was attended by over 200,000 people. In fact, even though Qualcomm stadium has hosted two Super Bowls and a World Series, none of those events hold the record for the largest attendance. That distinction is held by the Youth Night at the Billy Graham Crusade when 74,000 people attended.

● In addition, many area churches have experienced tremendous evangelism and growth, and a number of new churches have been planted.

● As I write this, these same churches in San Diego are spearheading an effort to change the state Constitution to define marriage as solely between a man and a woman. Our first assignment is to get 1.2 million signatures to qualify a ballot initiative.

And what of that little prayer group that began twenty years ago? Well, we still meet every Thursday morning. Some time ago, thirty-five pastors from the El Cajon area met for prayer in the city council chambers with our mayor and a city councilman (both of whom are born again) to pray in agreement for our city and to hear our mayor declare that El Cajon belongs to the Lord Jesus Christ. Truly, united prayer is working a marvelous thing!

The Bible tells us that we *"have been made complete"* in Christ, and that *"He is the head over all rule and authority"* (Colossians 2:10). Further, it goes on to tell us that He has *"disarmed the rulers and authorities"* (Colossians 2:15). Let us boldly and obediently follow Christ in displacing these powers from over our cities.

Our cities are waiting for us to agree with heaven and displace these evil powers, and thereby release deliverance and freedom to our communities.

DISPLACEMENT WITHIN AN INDIVIDUAL

The principle of displacement operates on the cosmic or universal level, and also on the personal one. Do you remember Jesus' words to the Israelites which we quoted earlier?

> *Now when an unclean spirit goes out of a man, it passes through waterless places seeking rest, and does not find it. Then it says, "I will return to my house from which I came"; and when it comes, it finds it unoccupied, swept, and put in order. Then it goes and takes along with it seven other spirits more wicked than itself, and they go in and live there; and the last state of that man becomes worse than the first...*
>
> (Matthew 12:43-45)

Just like nations, individuals can reject one deception only to fall into a far worse one. How many people have rejected an empty and legalistic Christianity only to fall victim to something far worse? For example, John, one of my childhood friends, rejected the legalism of his church, and has spent the last thirty years in stagnation, apathy, marijuana, alcohol and a curious smattering of Eastern thought.

During the '60s and '70s, a generation rejected a hollow and hypocritical Christianity and shallow national conformity. However, seven devils far worse have taken their places and brought devastation to many lives.

Sometimes people will escape Mormonism or Jehovah's Witnesses or some other cult, only, in their emptiness and hurt, to fall into something worse - like addiction or adultery. The goal should never be to simply bring someone out of a deception and then leave them empty, vulnerable to a worse deception. The goal must be to displace the deception with the Gospel of the Truth of Jesus Christ! We can spend too much time trying to convince people that Mormonism is wrong rather than that biblical Christianity is right. If we convince them of the falsehood of Mormonism without also convincing them of the truth of Christianity, have we really done them a favor?

If we want to help people change, we must realize this fact: People will resist change because they are afraid that what might come is worse than what they have presently.

People prefer the devil they know to the one that they don't.

I have found people will hold onto their lifestyles, no matter how dysfunctional, rather than face the unknown consequences of change. They will stay in abusive relationships; they will continue their dependency on drugs and alcohol rather than launch off into the unknown.

People fear emptiness and loneliness more than anything else. We must help them to see that there is love, community and support waiting for them as they change. We must demonstrate that God and His Church are supportive of them. If they can displace their confusion with love and joy, they will not be left empty and alone.

Many people feel as I did once, when I realized my lifestyle was a mess. The friends I had were destructive, my philosophy of life was negative and worst of all, alcohol was my great crutch in life. Despite these problems, I was not ready to give up my lifestyle.

It was the only life I had, the only way I knew how to relate to things. As bad as it was, I resisted throwing it away, afraid of facing the challenges of life without them. I felt naked and empty inside. It wasn't until Jesus Christ filled my empty heart that I was able to throw off the old ways.

The Principle of Displacement is important in our efforts to change ourselves as well. Rightly understanding this principle is a key to our success or failure in seeing our own personal lives change. This is such an important area that we will examine it closely in chapter sixteen: The Kingdom Key of Inner Transformation.

The principle of displacement is an important parameter in our Creator's design of His Creation. It functions in every dimension, and is an important key for us to understand and employ in seeing the Kingdom of God triumph in every sphere of life. The following two chapters will focus on how this principle works in other spheres of life.

15

The Kingdom Key of Displacement: Part II

As we have seen, displacement is a principle that operates in both the physical and spiritual realms. Just as water displaces air from a glass, and light displaces darkness in a room when the door is opened, so, too, the Kingdom of God displaces the kingdom of darkness, and righteousness will displace unrighteousness.

The Principle of Displacement is a key God has given us to effect change. In the last chapter, you studied how the principle of displacement relates to heavenly realms; now, let us look at how it operates among the governments of mankind.

DISPLACEMENT IN EARTHLY AFFAIRS

In the same way that the Kingdom of God displaces resistant demonic spiritual authorities and powers, so, too, injustice and unrighteousness remain in place in earthly governments until they are displaced by a righteous order. Let us return to a scripture we studied earlier. Jesus told this story to make a point about the evil nation of Israel and its evil spiritual leadership.

> *Now when an unclean spirit goes out of a man, it passes through waterless places seeking rest, and does not find it. Then it says, "I will return to my house from which I came"; and when it comes, it finds it unoccupied, swept, and put in order. Then it goes and takes along with it seven other spirits more wicked than itself, and they go in and live there; and the last state of that man becomes worse than the first. **That is the way it will also be with this evil generation.***
>
> (Matthew 12:43-45)

We usually relate this passage to individuals, but Jesus extended it to an entire nation. The nation of Israel had repented through the preaching of John the Baptist. God had granted them the grace to repent of their backslidden and greedy ways. They emptied their lives and prepared themselves for the Messiah.

But when He came, they rejected Him. They asked Jesus to prove Himself with a sign. They were unwilling to accept His words or His great miracles. They rejected the hour of their visitation.

Because they had refused to be filled with the new wine, they were empty. The Kingdom of God would have filled them with freedom, righteousness and blessing. But they had rejected it.

As we know, a vacuum cannot remain.

Soon, all the old deceptions and destructions came sweeping back into their culture and society. Their racism, pride, presumption, rebelliousness and other assorted vices came back worse than ever before, plunging their nation into horrible civil war and revolution. As a result, there was famine and bloodshed. Eventually, because of the upheaval and social chaos brought about by the various factions, Jerusalem and Israel were completely destroyed some thirty-five years later in 70 A.D by the Roman General Titus.

The nation did not exist for almost 1,900 years, until it was reborn through the United Nations in May of 1948.

A UNIVERSAL PRINCIPLE

This same principle holds true for every individual, family and nation. If, for instance, Russia and the other nations that once made up the former Soviet Union do not accept the Gospel of Jesus Christ, a far worse fate will befall them than they had under Communism. The same demonic powers still loom over those countries, eager to bring destruction, violence, hatred and repression under the guise of some new system. If the truth is not given place in those countries, their future could be worse than their past. That is why western Christians are rushing to fill these nations with the Gospel of Jesus Christ (but ethnic hatred, radical Islam, paganism and lawlessness are eager to fill the void as well). The ethnic cleansing that took place in Bosnia, the war in Chechnya, as well as the violence that has happened in other countries once behind the Iron Curtain, demonstrate the danger.

The continent of Africa has also demonstrated this principle. During the nineteenth and early twentieth centuries, European countries colonized most of Africa. During their reign over these nations there was much suffering and injustice imposed upon the native people. Following the end of World War II, these nations began to gain their independence. Within a short period of several decades, almost all of Africa gained independence. The rules and government of the colonizing powers were removed.

However, the void left by the collapse of colonialism often brought in suffering and destruction far worse than what the people had known under colonialism. A few countries, like Kenya and Nigeria (which were already predominately Christian), were able to move relatively smoothly to self-government.

The Gospel of Jesus Christ had already conquered that land so bloodshed, terrorism and genocide could gain no entry.

Most other African nations did not have as large a Christian presence. When the devil of colonialism was lifted, seven devils far worse came in to occupy the void. African history for the past fifty years is a story of civil and tribal wars, genocide, bloodshed, imposed famines, brutal dictatorships and bloody coups. Names like Biafra, Sudan, Zimbabwe, Uganda, Angola, Somalia and Rwanda have become synonymous with suffering and brutality.

FRANCE AND AMERICA

Freedom and justice do not come by merely replacing one devil with another. An ungodly order must be replaced with a godly one for progress to be made. If we contrast the founding of America with that of France, we have a powerful illustration of this truth...and a sober warning.

America was a nation founded mainly by Christian people who were forced to leave Europe due to religious persecution. In addition, from 1735 to 1745, American colonies experienced a tremendous revival led by men like Jonathan Edwards and George Whitefield. Historians refer to this period as the Great Awakening. It was a period when Christian beliefs and practices became the dominant force in our culture.

When independence was declared in 1776, the colonies were predominately Christian. The Gospel of Truth had thoroughly conquered our land. Consequently, following the War of Independence, there was no additional infighting, reprisals or bloodshed. The Gospel of Jesus Christ had displaced the evil of colonial rule. The documents that they created - the Declaration of Independence, the Constitution and the Bill of Rights - reflected a biblical worldview and biblical values. These values have endured down through the generations until today.

France's history stands in sharp contrast to ours. In 1685, France made Protestantism illegal and closed all the Protestant churches. All preachers were expelled from the country. Nearly 300,000 Protestant Christians left or were expelled. The Catholic Church which remained was little more than a subsidiary and organ of the government.

Humanism became dominant in France under leading thinkers like Voltaire and Jean Jacques Rousseau who violently attacked Christianity in their writings. They both died in 1778, two years after the independence of America was declared and eleven years before the French Revolution which their ideas helped spawn.

In France, the monarchy was overthrown by humanistic democracy.

One devil was replaced by another.

Unlike America's smooth transition, France would experience six bloody overthrows of government in the next twenty-six years. The years 1792-1799 became known as the *"Reign of Terror"*; tens of thousands of nobles, priests and commoners were executed, often on the guillotine.

History has few more compelling examples of the contrast between the Spirit of Jesus, which guided the founders of America, and the spirit of humanism which guided the founders of the French Republic. America, however, has been in a process of turning from the Spirit of Jesus to the spirit of humanism. Already, humanism inspires and directs most of the institutions of our country.

How did this take place?

AMERICA UP FOR GRABS

In the U.S. during the '50s and early '60s, the national Judaeo-Christian consensus was visible everywhere, and was given lip service by nearly everyone. However, it was an empty, nominal allegiance, not heartfelt or deep (nowhere was this truer than in our nation's universities). Consequently, it began to be displaced in the '60s by a new dominant consensus.

The sexual revolution, eastern mysticism, western evolutionism and existential hedonism all came together to form a new national consensus called "modern humanism." For the past forty years, this system has dominated our nation. It has, however, grown tired and bankrupt, failing on its promises.

Its fruit has proved bitter, and is now on the brink of being displaced by a new national consensus.

God is giving His people a great opportunity.

However, just like ancient Israel, if we do not accept the Kingdom message, the fate of America will be far worse under some new ungodly system than it ever was under humanism's rule.

We Christians must begin now to build a society and social structure that will step in and displace failing and decaying humanism. We must restore families and develop educational systems and new standards for government and media.

Now is the time for us to rise up and not only expose the failed promises and lies of humanism, but even more importantly, begin to build a new God-given vision and Holy Spirit-inspired strategy and wineskin.

PREPARATION AND PLANNING ARE REQUIRED

It is God's desire to give the nation into righteous hands. He will not give this responsibility into the hands of those who are unprepared to receive it. He is looking for those who prepare themselves and build new God-inspired wineskins and structures that will adequately service and care for this great stewardship.

We must seek God's face and then arise and build as God transfers responsibility over to us. This is the same principle He followed in giving the Promised Land into the hands of the Israelites.

> *I will send hornets ahead of you so that they will drive out the Hivites, the Canaanites, and the Hittites before you. I will not drive them out before you in a single year, that the land may not become desolate and the beasts of the field become too numerous for you. I will drive them out before you little by little, until you become fruitful and take possession of the land.*
>
> (Exodus 23:28-30)

God would not drive those out who were caring for the land until the Israelites were prepared to take over that function of stewardship and responsibility. If the Israelites had been given more than what they were prepared for, the land would have reverted to being a wild, unconquered land.

It is the same today.

We must be prepared to manage what God wants to give us. God is calling His people to leadership. Leaders must have enough faith to lead. It takes no faith to criticize and find fault with humanistic institutions like public education, for instance. It takes faith to prepare to educate the children of our country. If we are to become the leaders God intends us to be, we must do more than be critics. We must build solutions we can offer in place of these failed institutions and ideas.

If we want to be the leaders of tomorrow, we must begin today by starting where we are, to work at solutions to problems right where we are. As we gain experience, knowledge and resources, we will be in a position to receive promotion into doing truly wonderful things in the future. It is only as we work towards success at smaller matters today that we will be prepared and positioned for great matters tomorrow.

A Recent Illustration: Educational Vouchers

We recently saw a clear example of displacement here in California.

A voucher initiative was introduced on the ballot that would have given parents a voucher for their child's education to spend at any school, public or private, that they felt would best meet their child's needs. Californians were angry about the state of our schools, and early poll results showed the initiative was favored three to one. However, by election time, the opponents, spending vast sums of money, were able to defeat the measure. They simply created fear in people's minds by creating pictures of seven worse devils that could rush in to fill the void. Their campaign slogan was "It's a risk we can't afford to take."

They did not have to defend the present state of education being offered (which is bad), they merely pointed out that there is nothing large enough in place to displace it.

If there had been more private and religious schools in place, running efficiently, then people's fears could not have been aroused, and the voucher measure would have passed easily.

People would rather have the devil they know than the one they don't.

People will displace something inferior with something better, but they generally will not replace something, no matter how flawed, with the unknown.

It would violate the principle of displacement.

Evangelical Christians must first be able to educate our own kids before we can expect to be given greater opportunities.

If we cannot provide for the educational needs of our children, and bring them up in a Christian worldview, why would God grant us greater responsibility?

We as Christians must simply wake up to our own greatness as the people of God. With the leading and grace of the Spirit of God in our midst, and the richness of the many forms of gifts that God has put in the Church, along with the power of prayer, we can do anything, and do it with excellence!

It is nothing but lukewarmness, fear and unbelief that cause us to think we can't improve on the secular and humanistic answers. It is nothing but a complete lack of spiritual discernment and unbelief that causes Christians to continue to support failed and anti-God institutions, believing they have no other choices.

Don't Curse the Darkness, Light a Candle!

It doesn't take any faith to find fault with our prisons and criminal justice system. However, if God were to bring that system down, what could we offer in its place?

Praise God for men like Charles Colson, founder of Prison Fellowship, who not only minister to people in prison, but also work on biblical strategies for criminal justice problems. The state and federal government, as well as governments of other nations, have engaged Prison Fellowship to conduct experimental programs with felons that are revolutionary and based on clear principles from the Bible. These highly-successful pilot projects have been based on the biblical teachings of restitution and reconciliation. Charles Colson is preparing a biblical model of criminal justice and corrections that can displace the current failing humanistic system of criminal justice.

In the same way, Christians are taking up the challenge of educating our young. Homeschooling is an example of Christian innovation which is based on the biblical conviction that it is the parents, and not the state, who are responsible for the education and socialization of their children. In addition, many other innovative models have sprung up to join the large Christian school movement.

I have been greatly encouraged by the efforts and example of a friend of mine.

The Christian school where my children were attending was closing down. We had only been able to afford to send our kids to that school because my wife was able to work there. For us, affording the full tuition of a Christian school was not realistic.

One of the other teachers and parents at the school, Linda Hansen, had been praying about a burden God had placed on her heart to someday begin a school that would be an innovative blend of homeschooling and a more traditional Christian school. This school would give an option to parents who could not afford a fulltime Christian school, and yet were unable or unprepared to fully assume the task of educating their children.

Neither Linda, nor my wife, nor any of the other parents involved had ever started a school, or even been credentialed as teachers. Their only experience had been teaching as homeschoolers, or teaching at an A.C.E. Christian school.

Without any money, they began to follow God and fulfill this dream.

You can imagine the great obstacles they had to overcome.

However, God provided the way, and by the time the next school year began they were ready for students. In just their third year they had over 100 students, many of whom would otherwise be unable to have an alternative to public education. That in itself was pretty impressive.

But the story does not end there.

The following year our church started a second school, patterned after the first. Several years after that, both schools added grades 9-12. The schools have continued to grow in numbers and excellence. All this because two mothers, without any money or even a place to meet, set out in faith. Soon others caught the vision and joined in, and now fifteen years later there are over 700 students in these two schools. Although this seems very impressive, it merely is representative of what God wants to do through people who will receive vision and have faith.

Multiple examples could be cited where God is giving people a vision for building a work, based on biblical principles which can displace humanistic structures and institution.

DISPLACING BAD IDEAS AND PHILOSOPHIES

Christians must develop a comprehensive worldview and integrated philosophical system. We can never hope to displace the devil of secular humanism, the bully of "politically correct speech," unless we present a comprehensive and compelling presentation of the Bible's view of all reality.

It is not enough to merely criticize, condemn or ridicule other belief systems!

We must lay out a well-reasoned, comprehensive Christian world-view!

God's wisdom, found in the Bible, is so much more sublime, reasonable and adequate to explain the facts of life as we find them than all the other rival systems. It displaced pagan thinking once already in Western history and will do so again.

THE END OF THE MATTER

The prophet Daniel was summoned to the court of King Nebuchadnezzar, the king of Babylon, to interpret a dream the king had. King Nebuchadnezzar was the first man to rule over a worldwide kingdom. The dream concerned a huge statue of a man made up of various elements and materials. Each different element and material symbolically represented a future great empire or nation that would arise in the flow of world history. Towards the end of the dream a profound thing happened. Listen as Daniel relates the dream:

> *You continued looking until a stone was cut out without hands, and it struck the statue on its feet of iron and clay and crushed them. Then the iron, the clay, the bronze, the silver and the gold were crushed all at the same time and became like chaff from the summer threshing floors; and the wind carried them away so that not a trace of them was found. But the stone that struck the statue became a great mountain and filled the whole earth.*

> (Daniel 2:34-35)

Daniel explained to the king what we can all see now as obvious. After his kingdom, three other kingdoms would arise (The Persian, Greek and Roman empires are all clearly symbolized in the statue). These kingdoms would all pass away. However, a future kingdom would arise, one that was not manmade (*"a stone was cut without hands"*). This kingdom would fill the whole earth until it had dispossessed all other kingdoms and realms.

This ancient dream gives us the clue to our world's past, present and future. The Gospel of Jesus Christ and His Kingdom are dispossessing all other kingdoms and filling the whole earth. Already Christianity is the largest and most influential religion or belief system on earth. It may have started out as a small stone, but it finishes as a large mountain, growing until it displaces everything. The King of this Kingdom is Jesus! Of Him, the Bible testifies:

Of the increase of His government and peace there will be no end.
(Isaiah 9:7, NKJ)

THE GLORIOUS TRIUMPH OF CHRIST

From that early Sunday morning when the tomb was found empty until today, Christ's Kingdom has continued to grow and displace all other kingdoms and powers. As Isaiah prophesied, there has been no end to the increase of His government or of peace.

Sometimes people, and even ministers, will talk as though the earth is worse than it has ever been. Only someone who is either ignorant of history or who ignores it can say that. Even a cursory comparison of the world of today with the world before Jesus shows that the world of His day was much more corrupt, violent, brutal, unjust and in the sway of demonic powers.

Today, most of the world has been freed from demonic superstitions, slavery and genocide. Where today, for instance, can people be found offering their children up on fiery altars to demanding demon gods?

Where do you find nations and whole races conquered and put into inhuman, forced labor? Slavery, which was once the lot of most of the world's population, is now almost unknown.

The irrefutable truth is that a far higher percentage of the world's population is living in peace and freedom, with enough to eat, than at any other time in earth's history. This is not to minimize the suffering, evil and injustice present in our world, but merely to point out that what Isaiah prophesied in Isaiah 9:7 is coming to pass.

Every century has seen an expansion of Christ's Kingdom and its resultant blessings for mankind. Today, Christians comprise a larger percentage of the earth's population than at any time, and the Church is growing faster than at any previous time. Wherever the Church spreads it brings deliverance, freedom and peace.

Christ has increased His rule and strengthened His Kingdom each and every century, and His spiritual enemies have been driven to more and more remote places and to weaker and weaker positions. Whatever end-time scenario you think you have worked out, it had better be able to deal with the clear teaching of Scripture outlining the growth and triumph of Christ's Kingdom, and the fact of the clear flow of world history for two thousand years.

If you have bought into somebody's interpretation of the last days that puts fear in your heart and lulls you into inactivity in terms of taking leadership for the future because "Well, we know that it is just going to get worse and worse anyway," then your theology needs to be reexamined. Too many Christians see their churches as defensive fortresses vainly trying to hold back an unstoppable tide, rather than Christ's mighty army continuing its long campaign of victory.

In our country, we have lost this perspective largely because of the recent decline of the Church due to its unfaithfulness. Christ, however, is ready to glorify and exalt the Church as it repents and pledges again its faithfulness.

In fact, He has already begun to do that. Right now He is visiting His Church with great grace. This decade has already witnessed great and unprecedented expressions of unity as tens of thousands of Christians gather to march in city streets, worship in great stadiums and pray in huge conferences.

A third great awakening may be stirring in the United States.

NEEDED: AN AGENDA FOR GOD'S PEOPLE

Christians must recover hope and boldness. God is requiring His Church, through His grace, to rise up from mediocrity, apathy and unbelief and accomplish His great works. We must remember that everything belongs to our God.

The earth is the LORD'S, and all it contains, The world, and those who dwell in it.

(Psalm 24:1)

"I will shake all the nations; and they will come with the wealth of all nations...The silver is Mine and the gold is Mine" declares the LORD of Hosts.

(Haggai 2:7-8)

Not only do all wealth and possessions belong to God, but so does all authority. He is the head over all authority, and all authorities serve only at His allowance.

In order that the living may know That the Most High is ruler over mankind, And bestows it on whom He wishes, And sets over it the lowliest of men.

(Daniel 4:17)

Let the name of God be blessed forever and ever, For wisdom and power belong to Him. It is He who changes the times and the epochs; He removes kings and establishes kings; He gives wisdom to wise men, And knowledge to men of understanding.

(Daniel 2:20-21)

The Bible is clear that not only is God the owner and ruler of everything; He also retains the right to give it to whomever He wants, even if this means redistributing it. Concerning His people who walk with Him in covenant loyalty, He says:

Now it shall be, if you diligently obey the LORD your God, being careful to do all His commandments which I command you today, the LORD your God will set you high above all the nations of the earth... [He] will bless all the work of your hand; and you shall lend to many nations, but you shall not borrow. The Lord will make you the head and not the tail, and you only will be above, and you will not be underneath.

(Deuteronomy 28:1, 12-13)

God's desire and plan is to entrust His possessions and authority to those who are trustworthy. Ever since the Garden of Eden, He has always been looking for humans who are faithful stewards. To them He will entrust power, authority and all His possessions.

Blessed are the meek, For they shall inherit the earth.

(Matthew 5:5, NKJ)

Yet a little while and the wicked man will be no more; And you will look carefully for his place and he will not be there. But the humble will inherit the land And will delight themselves in abundant prosperity.

(Psalm 37:10-11)

He has done mighty deeds with His arm; He has scattered those who were proud in the thoughts [imaginations, KJV] of their heart. He has brought down rulers from their thrones, And has exalted those who were humble.

(Luke 1:51-52)

Of Jesus it was prophesied while He was still a baby:

Behold this Child is appointed for the fall and rise of many...

(Luke 2:34)

Everything in the world, along with all power and authority, belongs to King Jesus. He is looking for faithful people to whom to entrust it. When His people are unfaithful to their covenant with God, then the blessings are lost and His people, as well as His possessions, fall into ungodly hands (just as He warned us - see Deuteronomy 28).

We need to learn to be a faithful covenant people who walk boldly in all of our Father's possessions!

The airways that carry radio and television broadcasts belong to God; our governments belong to God; all the gold and silver of our world belong to God.

Why should we let our inheritance be ruined in the hands of ungodly users? We must learn to dispossess that which belongs to our Father from the unrighteous.

GIVE GOD SOMETHING TO BLESS

God is not calling us to be critics, but architects.

It is easy to criticize the folly of ungodly ways, but God wants us to rise up and build new biblical models and strategies of education, social welfare, business, arts and media. He wants us to show the world true Christian families and Christian community.

We must give God something to bless.

God does not delight in cursing, yet most of what surrounds us in our country and our communities is under a curse because it opposes or fails to honor God. God is wanting us to get direction from Him and build something He can bless, something that will arise while all else is sinking. God wants us to rise up and become the head and not the tail. God calls to us through the prophet Isaiah:

Arise, shine; for your light has come, And the glory of the LORD has risen upon you. For behold, darkness will cover the earth, And deep darkness the peoples; But the LORD will rise upon you And His glory will appear upon you. Nations will come to your light...

(Isaiah 60:1-3)

In these important days, God wants to be our teacher and partner and show us great and mighty things. He calls out to His children:

...I am the LORD your God, who teaches you to profit, Who leads you in the way you should go.

(Isaiah 48:17)

I will instruct you and teach you in the way you should go; I will counsel you with My eye upon you.

(Psalm 32:8)

Call to Me and I will answer you, and I will tell you great and mighty things, which you do not know.

(Jeremiah 33:3)

A CALL FOR THIS HOUR

Right now, God is calling us to be His solution to a humbled and desperate nation and world. Let us be encouraged to follow the example of such groups as Habitat for Humanity, a Christian group that counts among its adherents former President Jimmy Carter. This organization works alongside low-income people to help them build homes. This volunteer organization has grown until it is now the sixth largest home builder in the nation! It is a powerful, Christian solution for dealing with poverty.

In addition, we have the good example of the Southern Baptist relief organizations that send hundreds and even thousands of volunteers to disaster sites to help victims rebuild.

We live in a time of unprecedented opportunity for the Church to rise up and fill the current void of leadership. Leaders today do not have any viable answers to offer, and the people know it. I challenge you to name one single social problem that a humanistic institution is solving.

Public education?

The welfare system?

Congress?

Prisons?

The so-called Mental Health Industry?

All of the above are examples of failing institutions that cannot solve today's problems. People are looking for help.

In our community, even the public schools, racked by after-school vandalism and saddled by budget constraints, are approaching the churches and asking us to start after-school on-campus programs. Our church alone has after-school Bible clubs on ten elementary public school campuses and fourteen public middle school campuses. A number of other churches in the area are doing the same thing.

In addition, our church operates four community teen centers named Youth Venture which include a membership club, academic tutoring and one-on-one mentoring. Additionally, we operate a bus ministry, apartment visitation, various youth groups, camps, a large youth conference, and two schools. As a result, every year, hundreds of our adults work very effectively with thousands of our area children and teens. In the same way, we began a very successful drug and alcohol rehab ranch, a street ministry to the homeless, a ministry to the mentally challenged and a prison ministry, as well as many other outreaches. These ministries built on biblical principles and manifesting the love of God and the power of the Holy Spirit *are* making a huge difference.

The Church in America presently has a wide-open door to influence and disciple this generation. Thousands of opportunities are present.

If the Church of Jesus Christ does not rise up and seize our God-given opportunities to step into the current void and provide the leadership of Jesus to our generation, what devil might rise up in our place? Whoever can solve the problem and give people hope will be granted the authority to lead.

What great vision and work might God be calling you and your church to do for His glory? Are you doing everything He has presently given you to the best of your ability? Are you praying and seeking His face for greater vision and revelation? This is God's challenge to you.

Remember that God's plan to bring blessing and completion to our planet began by planting a garden and then putting a man and woman in it to cultivate and keep it (Genesis 2:7-8, 15). As they were "fruitful and multiplied" and labored in the garden, the garden would become enlarged, spreading God's blessing. God's plan has not changed. What garden has God placed you in? What area of responsibility and opportunity has He given you? What vision or dream has He put on your heart? Where is He calling you to become fruitful and to multiply? As we serve and labor by faith in our "garden" God will displace the brokenness of our world with the blessing of God.

Christians have no business being pessimistic or critical. We can do more than light a candle...we are light itself because Jesus is in us and will lead us to bring healing and salvation to our world. The answer to the world's woes is the Kingdom of God, and Jesus has promised to build it in our midst.

16

The Kingdom Key of Inner-Transformation

And do not be conformed to this world, but be transformed by the renewing of your mind…

(Romans 12:2)

Have you ever considered how much time and money we Americans spend on trying to change? Think of all the self-help books sold, seminars and conferences attended, twelve-step groups held, and New Year's resolutions made. Consider the billions of dollars spent on psychiatrists, psychologists, and even gurus and hypnotists.

Americans move, change jobs, get makeovers, get married, get divorced and even have kids in the hope of changing themselves and their lives. However, they are largely unsuccessful because they are ignorant of the keys to true and lasting change that God gives us in His Word.

Have you ever wanted to change something about yourself?

Of course you have.

Everyone wishes they could make deep, significant and lasting changes in their personality, temperament or habits.

We all struggle against habits, vices, fears and failings. We all have cried out for change because we know that these and other problem areas can bring devastating consequences into our lives.

But change is hard. Given our need for transformation, it is not surprising that the world has chased after the hundreds of different, ineffective routes to change (if one were effective, the other hundreds would not be needed!).

What is so surprising and tragic is that many in the Church have run after the latest psychological fad when the true route to lasting change is in the Bible. We become like the ancient Israelites to whom Jeremiah prophesied:

> *For My people have committed two evils: They have forsaken Me, The fountain of living waters, To hew for themselves cisterns, Broken cisterns That can hold no water.*
>
> (Jeremiah 2:13)

Many people have forsaken the proven, Bible-directed, Holy Ghost-inspired way of change. Instead, they have left the living waters for some trendy broken cistern full of the brackish liquid of humanistic thought. These cisterns (ideas and philosophies) truly "don't hold any water," and soon are abandoned as people follow after the next "new thing."

Personal observation tells us that the humanistic programs for change have failed. Yet, real, lasting change, even at the deepest levels, is possible. There are keys in God's Kingdom that lead to personal growth and change. By learning and practicing them, you will see change in yourself, and can be used by God to help others to meaningful change and freedom. In this chapter, we will look at the three key biblical steps to personal change.

STEP ONE: TAKE PERSONAL RESPONSIBILITY

Watch over your heart with all diligence, For from it flow the springs of life.

(Proverbs 4:23)

YOUR HEART: THE SPRING OF YOUR LIFE

The Bible clearly says that the key to the quality of your life lies in the condition of your heart. If we think of your life as a river, then the depth and direction of its flow is determined by the spring, your heart. The above verse could be supported with hundreds of other passages and verses that state this same truth. The decisive issue over your life is not your present circumstances or environment, not your past upbringing or past experiences...it is the condition of your heart. Your heart is the wellspring out of which your life will flow for better or worse.

This simple truth must be stated over and over again because of the deluge of humanistic philosophy and psychology that would bury this truth, even in the minds of Christians, beneath a landslide of wrong theories and opinions.

The Word says we are to watch (or guard) our hearts.

This puts the responsibility squarely on us!

The state of our lives is our responsibility.

Much of human secular thought wants to make victims out of us all and place the blame for everything we do on someone else. This philosophy has been guiding our social engineers for the past thirty years, and has been the approach of our schools, courts, welfare and correctional institutions.

What has been the result?

Seemingly, few are helped to a better life; instead society becomes more and more miserable.

On the other hand, a few groups and institutions have had some success in helping people by placing responsibility back on the individual. For instance, Alcoholics Anonymous, although it falls short of the total biblical route to lasting change, owes much of what success it has had to stressing individual responsibility. Recovery depends upon admitting your problem, coming out of denial, and taking responsibility for your actions (even making restitution where you have failed others). This contradicts most modern counseling, yet it is far more effective than other secular programs.

Blaming parents, society, environment or genetics has not produced the desired results.

If you would like to see your life transformed, the first principle you must embrace is the principle of personal responsibility.

You must quit blaming others for your present life, no matter what they have done. You must forgive them and take responsibility for your own changes. Until you do, you will have no real hope for change since you see yourself as merely the product of others' decisions and actions.

You must come to the place where you take responsibility for your thoughts, feelings, words and actions. It is, after all, you, and no one else, who is doing the thinking, feeling and acting.

Until you admit you are responsible, you cannot hope to change.

You can only change if you have the power of choice. Blaming others only casts you as a victim who is not responsible for your actions (and therefore unable to change).

STEP TWO: THE PRINCIPLE OF DISPLACEMENT

Everyone faces an inner battle (which is often secret). This is the battle to change ourselves, to eliminate secret sins and persistent failings.

All of us are familiar with the inner struggle of aspiring to a life that is lofty, courageous and noble, and of our frequent failures to do so. We know well the struggle referred to in Romans 7.

For the good that I want, I do not do, but I practice the very evil that I do not want. But if I am doing the very thing I do not want, I am no longer the one doing it, but sin which dwells in me. I find then the principle that evil is present in me, the one who wishes to do good. For I joyfully concur with the law (or rule) *of God in the inner man, but I see a different law* (or rule) *in the members of my body, waging war against the law* (or rule) *of my mind and making me a prisoner of the law* (or rule) *of sin which is in my members.*

(Romans 7:19-23)

Human nature is tragically flawed and weak. While we are often able to recognize the good and right, left to our own devices we are frequently unable to accomplish it. We often do the very things that we hate. Whether it is drinking, smoking, overeating, gossiping, boasting or worrying, we feel compelled to be defeated by them over and over again, even though we desire freedom.

WHY WILLPOWER IS SO WEAK

Most people try to change through willpower. They focus on their problem and try to eliminate the habit or shortcoming through a determined struggle of the will against the urge to continue it. The results of such resolutions and attempts are often failure, guilt and discouragement. If you are honest with yourself, you know that many attempts at lasting change have failed. Your will, like the rest of your being, is twisted and weakened by sin.

The Bible does not point us toward willpower as the hope of lasting change. Your will is part of your fallen human nature. You cannot use your fallen human nature to overcome your fallen human nature.

The harder you try not to do something, the more irresistible it seems. That is why food will never look or smell as good as when you are on a diet, and why temptations become stronger the more you try not to think about them.

The more you try not to do something or not to think about something, the more you focus on it and make it the center of your life. By focusing on the temptation, you actually energize your fallen human nature to be bound by it. For example, if a man tries not to think about pornographic images he has seen, he will find they keep flashing back into his mind. The more a woman tells herself not to think about her worries or fears, the more they seem to dominate her thinking. She finds she cannot get away from them and they drive her to distraction.

This is what Paul is talking about in Romans 7 when he writes:

For while we were in the flesh, the sinful passions, which were aroused by the Law, were at work in the members of our body to bear fruit for death.

(Romans 7:5)

Here we read that our sinful passions can actually be aroused by the Law. In other words, when we hear "thou shalt not" our attention becomes focused on the forbidden thing and our lust for it can be inflamed. By becoming front and center in our minds, the sinful allure of the forbidden thing is enhanced.

This is one reason why willpower alone, along with all its restrictions and prohibitions, cannot change us.

Why…do you submit yourself to decrees, such as "Do not handle, do not taste, do not touch!" These are matters which have, to be sure, the appearance of wisdom in self-made religion and severe treatment of the body, but are of no value against fleshly indulgence.

(Colossians 2:20-21 23)

The Bible teaches what human nature validates. Simply telling yourself not to do something does not work. The harder you try not to do something, the more powerful the urge becomes. Willpower and strict treatment of the body do not bring about lasting change. You may temporarily suppress problem areas, but at just the wrong time they can come roaring back to defeat you again.

Our human nature (including our will) was weakened and twisted by sin. We are simply unable to follow through on commands to change. Our fallen human nature cannot change our fallen human nature.

God had to supply us with a new way to change.

For what the Law could not do, weak as it was through the flesh, (that is our fallen human nature), *God did: sending His own Son…*

(Romans 8:3)

God's Law, His commandments, pointed the way to right living. The problem was that our fallen willpower cannot follow them. The Law therefore fails. Willpower alone cannot bring about right living.

GOD'S PLAN SUCCEEDS WHERE WILLPOWER FAILS

But God did not give up on us!

God's plan to change our lives is not to improve or perfect our fallen human nature, but to displace it with something else. He displaces our old nature with a new God-given nature. Any theory or therapy that attempts to patch up and heal our fallen nature, therefore, is bound to fail. If God Himself cannot fix our fallen nature, how can anyone hope to?

God gives us a new nature that is not corrupt and weak. The Bible teaches that this new nature is the very nature of His Son who is given to us when we are born again by receiving Jesus as our Lord and Savior.

Therefore if anyone is in Christ, he is a new creature; the old things passed away; behold, new things have come.

(2 Corinthians 5:17)

God's way is to displace the old nature with a new nature.

God's way rejects the old nature with its pride, insecurities, deceitfulness, weaknesses and compulsions.

This is far more radical than what most people expect. They simply want to be delivered from some aspect of their old nature - such as a violent temper or alcoholism. They just want to pull some weeds out of their old nature.

But Jesus knows the ground itself is bad. Weeds will forever be growing out of that old soil.

The soil itself must be changed!

All of our compulsions and failings are rooted in our old nature. We not only need deliverance from bad habits, we need deliverance from our fallen nature.

The Bible teaches us to consider our old nature dead (inoperative) through Christ, and declare that His new nature is fully operative in us now.

> *I have been crucified with Christ; and it is no longer I* (my unregenerate old nature) *who live, but Christ* (my new nature) *lives in me; and the life which I now live in the flesh I live by faith in the Son of God...*
>
> (Galatians 2:20)

DISPLACEMENT: PATHWAY TO CHANGE

Displacement is the daily pathway to change.

Change comes about as I daily seek to displace the thought patterns, ambitions, inclinations and longings of the old nature with the new nature given to me by Jesus.

This is really nothing more than repentance.

As I give place to the practices of the new nature, the old nature, with all of its weakness and sin, is itself weakened and displaced.

This is a very practical and workable plan.

I must realize that I cannot effect deep and lasting changes in myself by focusing my willpower on problem areas and overcoming them. I only energize them by giving them attention. But, I can overcome them by displacing them with a practice of the new nature.

I can overcome depression, not by telling my old nature not to feel depressed, but by displacing the depression of the old nature with some expression of the new nature. For instance, I can praise and thank God, singing worship to Him. In the same way, I can overcome selfishness by serving others in the power of the Holy Spirit. By so doing, I will yield to the new nature and gain freedom over the old nature.

That, in reference to your former manner of life, you lay aside the old self, which is being corrupted in accordance with the lusts of deceit...and put on the new self, which in the likeness of God has been created in righteousness...

(Ephesians 4:22, 24)

Until our hearts truly grasp this truth, and we abandon all humanistic attempts to bolster, patch up or reform our self-lives, we cannot truly change and please God. Our self-lives, with their identity, pride, self-interest and fears, are not the ground from which change can grow.

The old sinful nature within us is against God. It never did obey God's laws and it never will. That's why those who are still under the control of their old sinful selves, bent on following their old evil desires, can never please God.

(Romans 8:7-8, The Living Bible)

Any attempts to change that do not spring forth from our new nature, empowered by God's own Spirit, are doomed to fall short.

True, lasting and profound change is made by displacing the structures and processes of the old nature with the new. God has given to us His own Spirit so we might be empowered to change.

But I say, walk by the Spirit, and you will not carry out the desire of the flesh (your old nature) (Galatians 5:16).

Yes, the Bible tells us not to do certain things. But more importantly, it also tells us to drive out flesh-driven activities with Spirit-empowered activities.

Many places in the Bible spell out how to displace flesh-driven activities with Spirit-driven activities of our new nature.

Ephesians 4 is especially instructive in this.

	Flesh-Driven , Old Nature	Spirit-Powered , New Nature
v22.	Lay aside old self	Put on the new self (v24)
v25.	Laying aside falsehood	Speak truth
v28.	Let him who steals,	Let him labor in order that he might have something to share
v29.	Let no unwholesome word proceed from your mouth	But only such a word as is good for edification
v31.	Let all bitterness and anger...be put away from you	Be kind to one another, tender-hearted, forgive one another

There are many other places in the Bible with recipes for displacement. For a good study, go through 1 Peter, Romans 12 and Galatians 5.

MAINTAINING THE RIGHT FOCUS

The real focus of our will must be on a continual turning to God and an openness to walking by the Spirit. Instead of focusing on temptation, we must focus on the will of God so it may be accomplished in our lives. In this way, the nature of Jesus Christ within us will come to displace our fallen nature, thereby driving out temptation and sin. While our will alone does not have enough freedom or strength to withstand sin and habit, it can - with the power of the Holy Spirit - turn towards Jesus who will deliver us from every temptation.

Today, if you are being overcome by a poor self-image, do not, by an act of your will, stand in front of a mirror and tell yourself that you are beautiful and wonderful. This bad advice given out by some psychologists has no power to deliver you.

Rather, displace the old nature (which is self-focused) by reading God's Word. Learn about the wonderful work God has put into every individual (try Psalm 139 or Ephesians 2), and then thank and praise Him for His goodness and Wisdom.

Next, find scriptures about the call and purposes of God. Since you are one of His children, these scriptures will help explain God's purpose for your own life. Read Matthew 5:13-14, John 1:12; 15:15-16; 2 Corinthians 5:18-19, and then thank Him for His generosity in giving you such an exalted position!

When you rejoice in God's purpose and plan for your life, you will displace the self-love, insecurity and self-pity of the old nature with the gratitude and joy of your new God-given nature.

Follow this principle and your life will change.

Do you struggle with fear and anxiety?

Stop struggling against fear and worry.

The Bible tells you to displace them.

Be anxious for nothing, but in everything by prayer and supplication with thanksgiving let your requests be made known to God. And the peace of God, which surpasses comprehension, will guard your hearts and your minds in Christ Jesus.

(Philippians 4:6-7)

Notice that we are to displace fear and worry with prayer and thanksgiving and, as a result, God's peace will rule in our hearts and minds. This is the biblical way to change. For every failing in your life, find the opposite virtue in your new nature and begin to focus on it and practice it through the power of the Holy Spirit. Your life will profoundly and permanently change.

Do not be overcome by evil, but overcome evil with good.

(Romans 12:21)

This is a profound yet simple truth. I have seen it transform hundreds of lives, including my own, even where everything else had failed.

In my own life, as I wrote earlier, I had reached a point where I was an alcoholic. Nearly every night I was at a bar or a party, and I struggled with dark thoughts and deep depression. One night, at a church, I received salvation and the gift of the Holy Spirit.

God's light and love replaced the darkness and emptiness…but it didn't end there. The nightly visits to the bar were replaced by being at church nearly every night. Being drunk on alcohol was replaced by being filled daily with the Holy Spirit through worship and praise. The dark, self-focused thoughts were replaced by God's Word and a hunger for God's purposes and glory. Although no one had explained the Principle of Displacement to me, I had stumbled onto it in my zeal and gratitude to Jesus. This explains why the worst sinners often make the best saints. They embrace wholesale change in their lives.

STEP THREE: RENEWING OUR MINDS

By now you may be wondering, "What is the key step in unlocking the power of spiritual displacement in my life?"

The answer is in Ephesians 4:22-24:

That, in reference to your former manner of life, you lay aside the old self...and that you be renewed in the spirit of your mind, and put on the new self...

(Ephesians 4:22-24)

Note that between "putting off the old self" and "putting on the new self" lays a very important step. That step is *"that you be renewed in the spirit of your mind."*

Romans 12:2 echoes this same thought when it tells us:

And do not be conformed to this world, but be transformed by the renewing of your mind...

(Romans 12:2)

The key in displacing the old man with the new man is our mind.

The mind, the data center of our lives, is essential to our success. It supplies our will with the information to make choices and decisions. Wrong information will generally lead to wrong choices and decisions.

THE BATTLEGROUND OF THE MIND

When it comes to Christians moving out from defeat to victory and fruitfulness, without question, the mind is the principle battleground.

Whoever controls the mind will control the behavior.

People act according to what they perceive reality to be. If they believe they are helplessly locked into a condition, they will not attempt to get out of it. Choices will be limited by what they believe are the available possibilities.

If a person is unaware that Christ can give them a new nature that will displace the old nature, they may decide that change is impossible, give up, and simply begin to justify or rationalize their actions. You see, people either conform their desires to the Truth or else they will seek to conform the Truth to fit their desires. This is why so many in our country have tried to normalize sin and perversity. They have lost hope that they can change.

Until a person knows and is convinced of the truth of what Christ has done on their behalf, and of the new nature and identity available to them, they can never know freedom. This is why Jesus said:

If you continue in My word, then you are truly disciples of Mine; and you will know the truth, and the truth will make you free.

(John 8:31-32)

It is the Truth that grants you the opportunity to live in freedom! And it is only the Truth that allows us to live in freedom.

Many people seek religious experiences to validate their faith. Religious experiences are good, but no mere religious experience or fantastic emotional feeling with God will allow us to live in freedom. It is accepting and grasping the Truth and living in its reality that brings true freedom.

The opposite is also true. Rejecting God's Truth leads to bondage.

The Bible says that unbelievers live enslaved to sin and lusts and are *"excluded from the life of God"* because they *"walk, in the futility of their mind, being darkened in their understanding"* (Ephesians 4:17-18).

TRUTH OR CONSEQUENCES

Truth brings with it the possibility for freedom. Ignorance and deception lead inevitably to bondage and destruction. For this reason Satan is called "a liar and the father of lies" (John 8:44). By keeping people from the knowledge of the Truth, and the disseminating of lies, distortions and half truths, Satan tries to keep people in bondage. If people do not know the truth about their identity in Christ, their forgiveness from sin and guilt, and their new nature and its ability to displace their old nature, then the pathway to freedom is blocked.

Even if a person is born again and becomes spiritually alive by having Jesus dwell with their reborn spirit, they can still dwell in bondage and defeat. If their mind is filled with lies and deception, they will continue to live in defeat because their view of reality is warped. Their old nature will continue to dominate their life because they do not know that it can be different.

I once worked with a young man who had come from a very destructive background. His upbringing had caused him to have a warped view of himself and life. I led him to Christ, baptized him, delivered him from demons, led him to be filled with the Holy Spirit, taught him how to truly worship, expressed unconditional love to him and spent countless hours with him.

However, he continued to fall again and again, and to struggle with drugs.

It was not until his thinking was changed and he completely replaced his old identity with his new identity in Christ that he was completely set free. It was not until he began to act based on God's unchanging Truth rather than his feelings that his new God-given nature was able to displace his old nature.

This process took four years.

Being born again and filled with the Holy Spirit gave him the potential to change and be free, but it was only when he truly believed the whole Truth that he was free.

Only the Truth of God can set you free!

Being sincere can't do it. You can be sincere, but if you sincerely believe a lie, you will not be free.

Good intentions are not enough either.

It is not enough that you love God.

Only living according to the Truth of God's Word can bring about true change!

The Bible warns us that even God's followers can fall into bondage and destruction because of a lack of knowledge of the Truth.

Therefore My people go into exile for their lack of knowledge...

(Isaiah 5:13)

My people are destroyed for lack of knowledge...

(Hosea 4:6)

COMMITTED TO THE TRUTH

Even as God's children, we can only be free if we make a solid commitment to learning and following the Truth. You must commit yourself to Truth at any cost. You must say "I will believe and obey the Truth of God's Word over my feelings or natural inclinations." Only as we live by Theology rather than feelology can we live in freedom and truly change.

For instance, God's Word says:

If we confess our sins, He is faithful and righteous to forgive us our sins and to cleanse us from all unrighteousness.

(1 John 1:9)

Until you believe and are committed to holding to this truth no matter what, you cannot be free. You must hold on to God's Word even when the devil condemns you and even when you are assaulted by feelings of shame and guilt. You must believe that you are forgiven because God has promised it to you. Only if Satan can get us to doubt our forgiveness and the reality of our new nature can he hold us in defeat and shame.

The devil says "Look at you - you'll never change. You still have angry feelings and you are still tempted by terrible lustful thoughts. That's just the way you are. You'll never be anything else."

Satan wants us to believe that we are defined by our feelings and temptations.

On the contrary, the Bible says that we are defined by what we believe and what we *choose* to do - not what we are *tempted* to do. It is not our temptations that define us but our choices.

Unlike evolutionary humanism, the Bible does not view us as animals who are defined by animal urges, but rather as spiritual beings who define ourselves by our moral choices. The Bible says that we are not defined by our bellies (i.e. our appetites and urges) but by our hearts (i.e. our convictions, values and choices). In other words, having homosexual temptations and thoughts does not make us homosexuals and having violent dreams does not make us murderers. We will define ourselves by how we choose to act and live.

In order to be who we really are (who God says we are), all of us must be willing to resist certain sinful urges and temptations rather than surrender to them. Giving in to these urges does not bring us closer to "discovering who we really are," but actually takes us farther away from our true selves and makes us slaves. Only when we choose to live in truth and freedom can God reveal to us who we truly are and what are the plans He has for us.

The Bible teaches us to accept God's Truth (as found in the Bible) and to make our commitments and choices on the basis of that Truth. In so doing we define who we are and God's Spirit brings about true change in us. This is the difference between living like an animal and living as a free moral and spiritual being made in the image of God.

This means that all of us are free to change and grow if we will simply take God at His Word and be willing to live in the light of His Truth and promises.

You must believe, honor and follow God's Word above all other words or feelings. This is what it means to make a commitment to the Truth.

It is not enough to profess that the Bible is true, or to believe it sometimes. This will not make you free.

Look at what Jesus said.

If you continue in My word, then you are truly disciples of Mine; and you will know the truth, and the truth will make you free.

(John 8:31-32)

Jesus said that we must abide!

The King James translates that Greek word as "continue." If we would be free from our old habits and nature, we must continue in Christ's words at all times.

We cannot waver back and forth.

In the end, it all comes down to this simple question: Who are you going to believe?

Whoever we believe will be our master.

If we believe our feelings, emotions and urges then we will become their slave.

If we believe the devil and the world, then they will be our master.

But if we believe God's Word always, then He will be our Master and He will lead us into freedom and He will displace our old nature with our new nature.

Unbelief or Low Self-image

The world says our problems are caused by low self-esteem, anxiety disorders, clinical depression, a deprived childhood or a host of other reasons.

The Bible simply says our problems are caused by unbelief.

Unbelief is an unwillingness to accept God's Word concerning us, or a failure to live in response to that Word. If we would accept God's Word and base our thoughts, feelings, words and actions on it, then we would be free. Our new nature would displace our old nature; our new feelings would displace or replace old feelings, new actions would displace old actions, and new attitudes, old ones.

We must be committed to practicing the Truth.

Too many Christians hear the Word of God preached on Sunday, but forget it by Sunday night or Monday morning. We must study, practice, memorize and continue in God's Word if we are to be free.

I shall not forget Your word.

(Psalm 119:16)

Your word I have treasured in my heart, That I might not sin against You.

(Psalm 119:11)

A Changed Life: Why Not Start Today?

A changed life is available to each of God's children, no matter how damaged the upbringing or how sinful the past. It is an inheritance from God.

Change, however, must come through God's method and not through some trendy, humanistic theory. Remember, the three steps to godly change are:

● Take responsibility for your faults.

● Commit to displace your old nature with your new, born-again nature.

● Commit to the Truth of God's Word as the mechanism for transformation.

Why not begin the process of change in your life today? Remember, God's power is available to you right now if only you will follow His way as outlined in His Word.

Probing Deeper

Chapter 2

The Secret Keys to the Kingdom

Probing Deeper

1.   What evidences do you see that there is an invisible realm penetrating and influencing the physical world?

2.   Do you think most Christians take spiritual laws as seriously as the physical laws? Do they live as consistently in adherence to spiritual law as they do to natural law? Give examples to support your opinion.

3.   How would you rate your knowledge of spiritual laws? How many do you think you can identify? Come up with as many cause-and-effect spiritual laws as possible. (Here is a clue: Many of the promises of the Bible are actually statements of spiritual law; for instance, "Give and it shall be given to you," and "But if you do not forgive men, then neither will your heavenly Father forgive your transgressions."). Compile a list of as many as you can.

4.   What examples can you give from your own life or observations of spiritual laws operating in people's lives? These can be positive examples of how, by following the law, you or someone else benefited; or a negative example of how, by not following the law, it resulted in hurt or loss to the person.

Putting the Principle to Work

This week try to observe and write down as many examples of spiritual laws operating as you encounter. If you are reading through this book with a group of other Christians in a fellowship, be ready to share them at your next meeting.

Chapter 3

The Kingdom Key of Thanksgiving and Praise

Probing Deeper

1.   What do you think is meant by the following saying: "A thankful heart is not only the greatest virtue; it is the parent of all other virtues"?

2.   Look at Romans 1:21-32. How does this passage throw light on the maxim: "Ingratitude is the queen of all sins"?

3.   Developing an attitude and practice of thanksgiving is a powerful spiritual weapon to displace carnal, self-defeating attitudes that many of us struggle with. Discuss how developing a lifestyle of thanksgiving can eliminate the following bad attitudes:

      a.   Fear and insecurity
      b.   Envy
      c.   Pride
      d.   Other

4.   Experiment with this principle by taking the last five to seven minutes of the meeting to give vocal thanks as a group. Try to be creative and specific in your giving of thanks.

Putting the Principle to Work

The principle of thanksgiving and praise is an easy one to begin to practice. It merely takes the decision to begin to develop and practice the habit of giving thanks to God throughout the day. One way to do this is to try the following exercise.

Three or four times a day stop and verbally thank and praise God for ten things. Try to thank God for different things during each of the three periods.

What might be some other ways of putting this principle into action in your life? Discuss possibilities together. Have some people share what their action plan might be.

Chapter 4

The Kingdom Key of a Hidden Life With God

Probing Deeper

1.	Society seems to teach us that our failure or success depends upon our environment. When someone fails or breaks the law, the tendency is to blame his environment or upbringing. Furthermore, most people feel they cannot rise above the limitations of their circumstances.

The Bible shows that the true cause of success or failure is found in the condition of the inner man - not in outward events or circumstances. The Bible teaches that before there is outward failure there must be individual, inward failure (moral and spiritual failure), and that inward success or purity leads surely to outward success. Read and discuss the following scriptures: Proverbs 4:20-23, Luke 6:43-45, Psalm 37:31, Mark 7:14-15, and Matthew 15:18-20.

2.	Many Christians become frustrated because, although they desire to respond in a Christ-like way to an intense trial or pressure situation, they find they do not. They are like people who try to imitate the moves of Michael Jordan on a basketball court without having put in the hours doing drills that Michael put in. To respond like Jesus, we must first live a lifestyle like His. Dallas Willard wrote: "Following 'in His steps' cannot be equated with behaving as He did when He was 'on the spot.' To live as Christ lived is to live as He did all His life - that is, adopting His overall lifestyle."

Jesus' lifestyle involved a number of practices to keep Him in close fellowship and communion with His Father, practices that today we often call spiritual disciplines. As a group, try to list as many examples from the New Testament as you can of Jesus' involvement in prayer, Scripture memorization, worship or other spiritual practices.

3.   Share some of your experiences with the spiritual practices, or share the examples and results of others you have observed in this area.

4.   Consider and discuss the following two quotations.

> "Superficiality is the curse of our age. The doctrine of instant satisfaction is a primary spiritual problem. The desperate need today is not for a greater number of intelligent people, or gifted people, but for deep people" (Richard J. Foster).

> "To undertake the disciplines is to take our spiritual lives seriously and to suppose that following Christ is at least as big a challenge as playing the violin or jogging" (Dallas Willard).

Do you agree or disagree and why?

Putting the Principle to Work

This week, begin a plan to start building into your lifestyle some of the spiritual practices used by Jesus. Discuss among yourselves some of the possibilities. Next meeting, be prepared to share some of your experiences, successes and failures.

Chapter 5

The Kingdom Key to Overcoming Faith

Probing Deeper

1.   Read the parable Jesus spoke in Matthew 25:14–30. Remembering that faith is a gift Jesus gives us, how does this parable illustrate active faith?

2.   Discuss examples from your own life, or from the lives of others, that illustrate active faith.

3.   The key to benefiting from this Kingdom principle is to be sure you are acting on faith and not mere presumption. Faith is built upon the Lord's will as it is revealed; presumption is when we try to substitute our will for His, and then try to exercise "faith" to try and bring it to pass.

   I cannot operate in Holy Spirit-empowered faith to bring to pass something that is outside of God's will. For instance, it might not be my Master's will for me to get a private yacht. Discuss within the group ways that you as an individual might determine what God's will would be in a particular situation, and thereby know how to begin to act in faith. If you get stuck, look up the following scriptures for help: Psalm 119:9,98-100,105; James 1:5-6; Hebrews 13:7,17; Proverbs 13:10; 19:20; 24:6.

Putting the Principle to Work

A.   List several areas in your life where you need to see a breakthrough from God. Let it be areas where you must exercise faith.

B.   Next, select at least one of the problem areas above. Put together a plan, in view of question number three, of how you can, to the best of your ability, determine what God's will might be in the situation. (Remember, you do not have to determine it as an absolute certainty. You simply determine it to the best of your ability, and then humbly allow God to bring in the necessary correction and adjustments as you proceed.)

C.   After determining what you believe to be God's will in the individual situation, pray and discuss with others what might be an appropriate, obedient, faithful action.

Next meeting, return to report what progress you are making in this area.

Chapter 6

The Kingdom Key of True Repentance

Probing Deeper

1.   The New Testament expands and deepens Old Testament themes on repentance.

In the Old Testament, the word most often translated for repentance is *shub*, which literally means "to turn back" or "return."

In the New Testament, the two most common words translated as repentance are *metanoeo*, which means literally "to change your mind," or "to change your thinking," and *metameloma* which literally means "a change of feelings" or "a change of heart."

What does the difference in the meaning of these words tell us about how the New Testament deepened and expanded the Old Testament teaching on repentance? Why do you think the New Testament requires a deeper level of repentance? What makes this possible?

2.   Can you give an example of how yielding to God's conviction and repentance enabled you to come into a place of receiving God's blessings and riches? Discuss this with your group.

3.   Are there any areas where you especially need the gift of repentance so you can begin to walk in God's divine enablement? Spend several minutes in quiet contemplation concerning these areas in your life. Perhaps some in the group would be willing to ask for others to pray for them as they seek God in this area.

Putting the Principle to Work

Conviction and repentance are two of the best friends we will ever have since they open the door to God's riches for us. However, they cannot really take hold and begin to bear fruit unless they are given the time to do so. Set apart four or five blocks of time this week to contemplate and meditate on your life or on certain troubling aspects to it.

During this time, use a concordance to consult Scripture concerning these areas. Spend time in prayer. Consider approaching a trusted, mature friend to share honestly with you concerning these issues. Pray sincerely that God would help you with deep conviction and enable you to see these areas changed.

Do not delay. Do it!

Chapter 7

The Kingdom Key of Deligence (or Perseverance)

Probing Deeper

1.   Consider the lives of famous people throughout history whom you particularly admire. How did the Kingdom principle of diligence and perseverance figure into their lives? Consider the lives of Abraham, Joseph, Moses, David, Elijah, Jesus, Paul and others from the Bible. Think about noteworthy Americans like George Washington, Abraham Lincoln, Thomas Edison, the Wright brothers, Martin Luther King or other contemporary figures. How did these principles figure into their lives?

2.   What evidence, both positive and negative, from your own life can you share that bears on this Kingdom Key? Discuss it within the group.

3.   Look up and discuss the following scriptures concerning diligence: Proverbs 18:9, Proverbs 11:27, Proverbs 12:27.

4.   God commands us to be diligent in our practice of the Word. Read the following two scriptures that relate to being diligent in the Word as individuals, families and societies. In reading them, note the definitions of diligence in the Word, and also the promises associated with it. Deuteronomy 6:1-9, Joshua 1:7-8.

Putting the Principle to Work

For this week, memorize as many scriptures relating to diligence found in this chapter as possible. Recite them to yourself throughout the week. Also, review several crucial areas of your life in view of what you have learned about diligence. Begin to think about some of the dreams in your heart and how the practice of diligence could make them a reality. Discuss your thinking with others. Ask God to begin to form a plan in your imagination that could diligently be put into action.

Chapter 8

The Kingdom Key of Prciprocal Returns: Understanding the Immutable Law of Sowing and Reaping

Probing Deeper

1.   Discuss examples from your life, and from the lives of people you know, or even use examples from the daily newspaper to illustrate this principle of reciprocal returns in action.

2.   Read 2 Corinthians 9:6-11. It is one of the most important teachings concerning the principle of reciprocal returns. List all of the different principles in this passage that relate to this Kingdom Key. What additional guidelines can you get from it? Are these promises limited to giving in the financial realm?

Putting the Principle to Work

Make a list of areas where you especially need a breakthrough in your life, or where you really want to move ahead and prosper. Ask God to begin to show you ways in which you can begin to be a giver in those areas so you can eventually reap a harvest. Remember, be patient, doing nothing from selfish motives, but rather for motives that glorify Christ.

Chapter 9

The Kingdom Key of Giving

Probing Deeper

1.   Jesus said, "It is more blessed to give than to receive" (Acts 20:35). Now that you have studied the secret of giving, try to come up with five concrete reasons why it is really more blessed to give than to receive. Discuss these as a group.

2.   Using your own life, discuss blessings that have come into your life through giving. You can cite examples from other lives as well.

3.   Some people believe that the requirement to tithe, unlike the requirement forbidding murder or adultery, is no longer in force in the New Testament. Discuss this in the light of scriptures such as Luke 11:42 and 1 Corinthians 16:1-2. Do you feel there are any scriptures to support their view?

Putting the Principle to Work

Take God at His word. "It is better to give than to receive" (Acts 20:35) and "Bring the whole tithe...test Me now in this...if I will not open for you the windows of heaven" (Malachi 3:10). Make a solemn commitment to the Lord today and begin to be faithful in your finances to the Lord, trusting Him for the final outcome.

Chapter 10

The Kingdom Key of Agreement and Unity

Probing Deeper

1.   In what ways have we seen the dynamic of unity, or lack of unity, affect our nation over the past twenty-five years?

2.   What are some things that cause us to be double-minded, unable to come to inner unity and single mindedness? What are some things that are lost when we are double-minded? What are some things we can do to restore ourselves to single-mindedness?

3.   What are some things that destroy or hinder unity in a family? What are some things that are lost when a marriage or family loses unity and agreement? What things can be done to build or restore unity in a marriage or family?

4.   What are some things that hinder or destroy unity in a church? What are some things that are lost when a church loses or fails to attain true union and agreement? What things can be done to build or restore unity in a church?

Putting the Principle to Work

Pray about an area of your life where you especially need to work to build or restore unity and agreement. Use ideas from the discussion generated by the questions above to help you begin to build true unity and harmony. Come prepared next meeting to share what breakthroughs are taking place.

Chapter 11

The Kingdom Key of Vision

Probing Deeper

1.   Read Amos 8:11-13. It speaks of a time of a famine of vision from God in the land. Do you believe that America is suffering from such a famine? What about the mainline denominations? Public education establishment? Other institutions? Give reasons and examples for those that you feel are without vision.

2.   Think about your neighbors, coworkers and people whom you see every day. How does what we learned by studying this Kingdom Key illuminate their situation? Think about how they spend their time...does it reflect a lack of vision for themselves and their families? If so, how?

3.   Share examples from your life, or from the lives of people you know, where receiving a vision was life-changing.

Putting the Principle to Work

Write down your major responsibilities. For instance, they might be: husband, father, church member, etc. Include in that list one, two or three major problem areas that have been burdens on your heart. For instance, discipline problems at your child's school, or low morale at your work, or street gangs are some of the possibilities. There is any number of possibilities. Begin to pray over all the items on your list and ask God in the weeks and months ahead to begin to give you vision for His purposes in those areas. Ask Him to give you His eyes to see as He sees all the items on your list. Ask God to let you see them with His possibilities and plans. Continue this prayer until you get it answered.

Chapter 12

The Kingdom Key of Inspired Imagination

Probing Deeper

1.   Romans 1:21 (KJV) explains the slide into depravity of mankind:

Because that, when they knew God, they glorified him not as God, neither were thankful; but became vain in their imaginations, and their foolish heart was darkened.

Note that, as a result of ingratitude, their imaginations began to be filled with vain imaginings. Note also that their hearts became darkened and deceived. How does ingratitude lead to the heart being filled with vain imaginations?

After answering the above question, explain how vain imaginations might lead to a darkening of the heart (i.e., a gradual deception and foolish reasoning). Do you see evidence of this in the people around you? Explain.

2.   Is imagination valued in our religious upbringing? If not, how might we bring this aspect of our being more into play in our relationship to God?

3.   Tell of a time that a dream, vision or something you saw in your imagination proved to be from God. What was the outcome?

4.   What might be the pitfalls of trusting our imaginations too much? How might we safeguard ourselves from this danger without abandoning the value of our imaginations?

Putting the Principle to Work

Take the list of things you have been praying over from the last chapter. Now begin to attach Scripture stories and promises to each one, and begin to meditate on these as you pray and think about the items on your list.

Meditate upon them throughout the day. Pray and muse on them from the perspective of God and His Word. Allow God to begin to paint in your imagination. Do not be impatient.

Chapter 13

The Kingdom Key of Submission: The Principle of Delegated Authority

Probing Deeper

1.   Why do you think many Christians have trouble submitting to authority in the Church, family and in their everyday lives?

2.   If someone has trouble submitting to authority, what should they do?

3.   How is this idea of spiritual authority related to the family?

4.   Has the Lord taught you any lessons concerning spiritual authority or submitting to authority that you could share with others?

5.   Further reading: Numbers 12: Aaron and Miriam criticized Moses; Miriam became a leper. Leviticus 10: Nadab and Abihu subverted Aaron's authority; they were consumed by fire.

Putting the Principle to Work

A.   Make a list of those individuals God has put in authority over your life, and prayerfully consider your attitude toward each person.

B.   TAKE ACTION! If you sense you need to repent to God for your attitude toward His delegated authority in your life, do so immediately. If you believe you need to be reconciled with someone who has or had authority over you, do it! Don't delay!

C.   Make a commitment to be respectful and submissive to those God has placed in authority over your life.

Chapter 14

The Kingdom Key of Displacement

Probing Deeper

1.   Can you name other examples of the Principle of Displacement at work in the world today? Try to find examples from the spiritual, physical and social realms. Do you think such a principle truly exists?

2.   The lesson stated that a positive building of the Kingdom of God should be given priority over "a defensive running skirmish against the advance of the supposedly invincible forces of Satan." Do you agree? Think of some examples of "defensive skirmishes" and examples of "positive Kingdom building" that are taking place in our society today.

3.   According to Ephesians 6:13-14, what are the first two requirements we must take up before we are able to stand against the spiritual evil of our day and defeat it? Why do you think these two are listed first? Discuss examples, both positive and negative, that illustrate the need for these two qualities in the victorious Christian life.

Putting the Principle to Work

Consider an area of personal importance to you where you have let sin or the devil set the agenda and you have been fighting a defensive skirmish. How can you begin to let God set the agenda in this area? Perhaps you might want to share it with the group, or one or two others for advice.

Chapter 15

The Kingdom Key of Displacement: Pt. II

Probing Deeper

1.   It was stated that "The current America worldview is dominated by secular humanism, and has 'grown tired and bankrupt,' on the brink of being displaced." Do you agree or disagree? What evidence can you give to support your view? What are some other "worldviews" which are waiting to fill the void?

2.   What are some ways in which Christians today can prepare themselves and begin to displace the secular-humanistic American worldview with a biblically-based, Christian worldview? What are some things we can do as individuals? What are some things we could do as churches?

3.   Read again Psalm 37:11. Can you find examples in your current personal life or our national and international situation that illustrate this truth?

Putting the Principle to Work

Make a list of ministries, projects, or Christian endeavors you know that are being used to build the Kingdom of God. Begin to pray for them and ask God what He would have you do to help them.

Chapter 16

The Kingdom Key of Inner Transformation

Probing Deeper

Read Galatians 5:16-26. It gives us a list of flesh-driven things that must be displaced, and a list of Spirit-driven things with which to place them. Go through the list of fleshly activities and give current examples of them. Don't be surprised if some of your examples may be currently accepted behaviors, or even politically correct. Also show the opposite, Holy Spirit-driven activity.

In Ephesians 4:22-24, displacement is defined as a three-step process which includes:

    a.   Put off the old self.

    b.   Be renewed in the Spirit of your mind.

    c.   Put on the new self.

Discuss how this process might be followed in dealing with some of the current problems people have. You might consider such things as foul language, drug use, jealousy, insecurity, etc. Take one at a time. Discuss what it might mean to "Put it off" (be thorough), discuss how one's thinking in the area might have to change to "renew the mind" according to God's Word. Finally, discuss how to "put on"or allow a new activity to displace it.

3.   Try, as accurately as possible, to outline the difference between the biblical pathway to transformation and the many current psychological models that promise change. What are the main underlying assumptions of each? Are there any points of agreement?

Putting the Principles to Work

List one particular fleshly behavior or sin in your life that must be displaced. Using the three-step process of Ephesians 4:22-24 (Put off, renew your mind, put on), develop a specific strategy for change. Be specific. What would it mean to "put off" behavior - what in your thinking would have to change to renew your mind by God's Word in that area?

How could you "put on the new man" or displace the flesh with Spirit? Put your strategy on paper and practice it daily.

About the Author

Mark Hoffman (B.A., Point Loma College, M. Div., Bethel Seminary West) lives in La Mesa, California, with his wife, Linda.

Along with his brother, Dave Hoffman, he co-pastors Foothills Cɪ   ˙an ʰurch in El Cajon, California, which they founded in 1985.

You can write to Mark Hoffman c/o:

Foothills Christian Church
350 Cypress Lane., Suite B
El Cajon, CA 92020
(619) 442-7728

To order more copies of *Unlocking the Kingdom*, please send $16.00 (plus ₊2.00 for shipping and handling) to the above address. On orders of 10 or more, please call for discount pricing.

Endnotes

1 Pat Robertson and Bob Slosser, *The Secret Kingdom*
       (Nashville: Thomas Nelson, Inc. 1982) 138.
2 Robertson 137–138.
3 George Barna, *The Power of Vision* (Ventura: Regal Books, 1992) 21.